How to Read
THEOLOGY

How to Read
THEOLOGY

Engaging Doctrine
Critically and Charitably

UCHE ANIZOR

Baker Academic
a division of Baker Publishing Group
Grand Rapids, Michigan

© 2018 by Uche Anizor

Published by Baker Academic
a division of Baker Publishing Group
PO Box 6287, Grand Rapids, MI 49516-6287
www.bakeracademic.com

Printed in the United States of America

Library of Congress Cataloging-in-Publication Data
Names: Anizor, Uche, 1976– author.
Title: How to read theology : engaging doctrine critically and charitably / Uche Anizor.
Description: Grand Rapids : Baker Publishing Group, 2018. | Includes index.
Identifiers: LCCN 2017051467 | ISBN 9780801049750 (pbk. : alk. paper)
Subjects: LCSH: Bible—Theology—Study and teaching. | Bible—Criticism, interpretation, etc. | Theology.
Classification: LCC BS543 .A536 2018 | DDC 230.072—dc23
LC record available at https://lccn.loc.gov/2017051467

Scripture quotations are from the Holy Bible, New International Version®. NIV®. Copyright © 1973, 1978, 1984, 2011 by Biblica, Inc.™ Used by permission of Zondervan. All rights reserved worldwide. www.zondervan.com

18 19 20 21 22 23 24   7 6 5 4 3 2 1

In keeping with biblical principles of creation stewardship, Baker Publishing Group advocates the responsible use of our natural resources. As a member of the Green Press Initiative, our company uses recycled paper when possible. The text paper of this book is composed in part of post-consumer waste.

To Dan Treier,
a model of the critical yet charitable reader

Contents

Illustrations

Acknowledgments

Several people contributed graciously to this project, which is better because of them. A special thanks to Hank Voss, Jordan Barrett, and Steve Pardue for thorough, thoughtful, and encouraging feedback on many portions of this book. Thanks to the LA "Inklings"—Charlie Trimm, Bob Lay, and Jeremy Treat—for feedback on an early chapter. Thanks to my colleagues Karin Stetina, Ryan Peterson, and Jason McMartin for helpful, critical comments on an early chapter. To Fred Sanders, Matt Jenson, and Dan Treier—thank you for the fruitful exchange of ideas regarding material in the later chapters of the book. Thanks to Garrett Eaglin for being the first to read the whole manuscript and giving me helpful feedback from a student's perspective. I am grateful to Biola University and Talbot School of Theology for a sabbatical in fall 2016 that helped me complete the project. To the wonderful folks involved in Biola University's Center for Christian Thought (CCT) in fall 2015—Nick Bogardus, Tom Crisp, Liz Hall, George Hunsinger, Klaus Issler, Steve Porter, Ellen Ross, Gregg TenElshof, Eric Silverman, and Rico Vitz—thank you for carefully reading the first chapter and providing valuable corrections and points for clarification. Indeed, parts of this book benefited from a research fellowship at CCT, which was made possible through the support of a grant from Templeton Religion Trust. The opinions expressed in this publication are those of the author and do not necessarily reflect the views of Templeton Religion Trust. To Dave Nelson from Baker, thanks for your excitement about this project as well as your patience and encouragement along the way.

Finally, Melissa, Zoe, Eli, and Ezra, as always you provide the most cherished context in which I do all my work. Thank you for your continued love and support.

Prologue

What Kind of Book Is This?

Mark Twain once wrote a letter to his close friend Reverend J. H. Twichell, reacting to a borrowed copy of Jonathan Edwards's great work *The Freedom of the Will*. In it Twain confesses, "I wallowed and reeked with Jonathan in his insane debauch; rose immediately refreshed and fine at 10 this morning, but with a strange and haunting sense of having been on a three days' tear with a drunken lunatic. . . . All through the book is the glare of a resplendent intellect gone mad—a marvelous spectacle. . . . By God I was ashamed to be in such company."[1]

What strong words about America's greatest theologian! Is this reaction warranted? Twain responds harshly to a Calvinism with which he was familiar and in which he was reared (to some degree as a Presbyterian). Even though he concedes that Edwards makes some sound points, Twain finds the book wanting. He sees in Edwards's work the signs of brilliance but must ultimately part ways with the

---

1. Mark Twain, *Mark Twain's Letters*, ed. Albert Bigelow Paine, vol. 2 (New York: Harper & Brothers, 1917), 719–20. Twain further comments, "No, not *all* through the book—the drunk does not come till the last third, where what I take to be Calvinism and its God begins to show up and shine red and hideous in the glow from the fires of hell, their only right and proper adornment."

theologian. What Twain illustrates, at the very least, is that theology calls for a considered response, even if one less violent than Twain's.

This book is about *reading* theology. It is for those who want to think carefully about the theology they read and who enjoy the task but are still developing basic skills. As such, it is meant to be a primer to theological texts that introduces readers to the "behind the scenes" happenings in those texts, helping them better grasp the meaning of what exactly they are reading when they read theology. This book is meant to help the students who suddenly realize that they, like Twain, need to make some sort of decision about what they are reading but may not know where to begin. More accurately, then, this book is about *evaluating* theologies. In writing it, I have sought to maximize readers' benefit from theological literature, especially texts with which they may have major disagreements. I am convinced that something special can be gained from most theological texts, but they must be approached the right way—that is, critically *and* charitably. To use a well-worn image, reading theology well involves engaging both your head and your heart.

To that end, the book is divided into two parts. Part 1 is concerned with helping readers foster a charitable disposition toward theological texts. Chapter 1 explores four antilove postures (or "enemies of love") that get in the way of charitable reading in theology. Chapter 2 contends that since theology is never conducted in a vacuum, some knowledge of a theologian's context (or "backstory") is crucial if we are to judge his or her work fairly. Becoming increasingly familiar with the story of the theologian or their theology will foster a sympathetic and discerning reading.

Part 2 aims to develop skills for reading theology critically. Developing these skills, however, should never be divorced from developing character. Moving from part 1 to part 2 does not signal a departure from charity to focus on critical reading. Rather, charitable reading, as I will suggest, is often the most intelligent reading, and reading is most critical when we attend to another's work closely, carefully, and with sympathy. Critical reading, properly understood, is reading done in love. The chapters comprising part 2 provide tools, but tools in the hands of the unloving can easily become weapons (for pigeonholing, quickly dismissing, and so on). With that in mind,

part 2 explores how theology relates to the other resources we possess:
Scripture, tradition, reason, and experience. Each respective chapter
examines how theologians have variously understood the relationship between theology and the resource in question and ultimately
asks how these resources might be used as criteria for assessing theologies. Chapter 3 explores scriptural authority, focusing mainly on
how to understand how the Bible is used and the authority it has in
doctrinal formulation, so as to provide more categories for evaluating
whether a theologian or theology is "biblical." Chapter 4 examines
the relationship between theological proposals and the Christian
tradition, particularly the importance of knowing the Christian past
for evaluating theology past and present. Chapter 5 addresses the
question of theology's rationality—its coherence and cogency. Finally,
chapter 6 explores how doctrine and experience should correspond.
When we read theology, we should ask at least two questions: (1) How
is this theology reflective of the experience of Christians presently
or historically? (2) What are the practical or ethical consequences
of following this theology? In chapter 6, I discuss experience as an
explicit criterion for evaluating doctrine.

To illustrate each of these points, I have sprinkled examples
throughout each chapter. I have deliberately kept these examples
brief, which seems appropriate given this book's length. Therefore,
it will be up to you, the teachers and readers of this book, to apply
the principles herein to your own small samples of theological texts. I
present a starting point, a guide for engaging doctrine, not a *summa*
on all things related to reading theology. May this guide sharpen your
vision that you might see what is there in theological texts, and may
it prepare you to engage in the discipline of reading theology with a
critical mind and a charitable heart.

PART 1

On Reading
CHARITABLY

1

Enemies of Love

The Challenge of Reading Theology Charitably

> To read with intelligent charity. . . . To read lovingly because of and in the name of Jesus Christ, who is the author and guarantor of love.
>
> —Alan Jacobs, *A Theology of Reading*

In his final lectures, Karl Barth sums up a lifetime of theological work, memorably describing his vocation in this way: "Evangelical theology is concerned with Immanuel, God with us! Having this God for its object, it can be nothing else but the most thankful and *happy* science."[1] Those who know the God of the gospel should need no convincing that theology—the contemplation of this God—has great value and is a source of great joy. Yet if we are honest, we recognize that as much as theology is the "happy science" in theory, many do not experience it as such. For example, Helmut Thielicke, in his

---

1. Karl Barth, *Evangelical Theology: An Introduction*, trans. Grover Foley (Grand Rapids: Eerdmans, 1979), 12.

famous *Little Exercise for Young Theologians*, locates the source of unhappiness primarily in the theological student. In a chapter titled "Unhappy Experience with a Theologian's Homecoming," he recounts the story of a young seminarian who returns home "horribly changed" after his first semester of formal training. The simple and passionate faith he once had was replaced by hubris resulting from the new and fascinating ideas he has learned. After three semesters he becomes effectively useless for ministry in the church, being unable to condescend to the level of the average layperson. "The inner muscular strength of a lively young Christian," Thielicke concludes, "is horribly squeezed to death in a formal armor of abstract ideas."[2] Pride, immaturity, inexperience—these can convert a happy science into a somewhat suspect discipline. For while the young theologian found some form of joy in theological study, the desired beneficiaries of his learning experienced his joy as misery.

One response to this unhappy state of affairs could be to ignore the supposed cacophony of erudite voices—that is, the study of theology—in favor of the simple melody of Scripture alone. But that option is not available to us. In fact, the happy science must be carried out by theological students of all stripes in learned dialogue with theologians of the past and present. That is, we must *read* theology. Indeed, Barth points out that theological study must consist of at least two conversations: a primary and a secondary. The first involves the student directly engaging with Scripture to discern what God is saying to her and her community in her time. Of the secondary conversation Barth writes, "The student must permit himself indirectly to be given the necessary directions and admonitions for the journey toward the answer which he seeks. Such secondary instructions are gained from theologians of the past, the recent past, and from his immediate antecedents—through examination of their biblical exegesis and dogmatics and their historical and practical inquiries. . . . No one, however, should ever confuse this secondary conversation with the primary one, lest he lose the forest for the trees."[3]

---

2. Helmut Thielicke, *A Little Exercise for Young Theologians*, trans. Charles L. Taylor (Grand Rapids: Eerdmans, 2003), 7–8.

3. Barth, *Evangelical Theology*, 174.

We come to know God as we converse with fellow readers of the Bible. Yet this is precisely where another set of problems emerges, not so much for church members (as in Thielicke's tale) as for the practitioners themselves. As a seminary student it was not uncommon for me to encounter a theological text and have absolutely no clue what to make of it. There was a strangeness to it, and it was not always evident how I could profit from it on my journey of faith seeking understanding. This sometimes resulted in frustration: with my professor for assigning such difficult and "unclear" readings, with the writer for being obscure or "unbiblical," and with myself for being dull and "missing something." My situation is not unique. I remember giving a brief lecture on liberation theology to upper-year Bible and theology majors where the students repeatedly asked, "So what?" They were uncertain how these black, feminist, and Latin American theologians could possibly be helpful to them, especially considering that (in their eyes) these theologians offered nothing discernibly biblical, or at least exegetical, in their formulations. Why spend time studying them? A fine question, I think, but somewhat misguided. On the one hand, the students were correct to assume that some writers are better guides into Scripture and the knowledge of God than others. On the other hand, they incorrectly assumed that if the text's value was not self-evident and immediately experienced, the theology had little worth. In light of these concerns, if we are to read theology, how might we engage it profitably?

What has become clear to me is that I, my students, and countless others face several barriers to understanding and assessing theologies well. Some of these challenges are skills-related, while others are tied to disposition. There are indeed things one needs to know and practices in which one needs to be skilled in order to read theology with understanding (and subsequent chapters will go some way in addressing those concerns). But our attitudes also influence how we read theology; they can be productive for or prohibitive to reading theology well, and for our purposes that means reading theology critically *and* charitably, or with "intelligent charity," as Alan Jacobs puts it. In this chapter we will, as a spiritual exercise of sorts, reflect on some dispositional obstacles to this kind of reading, reading that befits an evangelical theologian—one concerned to honor the God of the gospel.

Obstacles to Intelligent Charity

To love God and to love one's neighbor as oneself is an impossible task. Moreover, how does this all-encompassing command intersect with the particular activity of reading theology? Although the meaning of Jesus's twofold love command appears fairly straightforward, it does require some elaboration, particularly if we are to apply it to the act of reading theology.

The attempt to bring this commandment into dialogue with the reading of texts is no new thing. Augustine, applying Christ's twofold love command to the interpretation of Scripture, famously writes, "So anyone who thinks that he has understood the divine scriptures or any part of them, but cannot by his understanding build up this double love of God and neighbour, has not yet succeeded in understanding them. Anyone who derives from them an idea which is useful for supporting this love but fails to say what the writer demonstrably meant in the passage has not made a fatal error, and is certainly not a liar."[4] The point for Augustine is that a reading of Scripture is good if it *results* in love for God and neighbor. Love is not primarily the disposition or driving motivation in reading but more the outcome of proper interpretation, even if the interpretation is de facto wrong. Alan Jacobs, in *A Theology of Reading*, extends Augustine's inquiry into the field of literary hermeneutics, asking how Jesus's command might shape our reading of literature. What might it look like to read with "intelligent charity"? he queries.[5] His essay is an extended theological reflection on the obstacles and challenges to, and the promise of, reading texts charitably. My concern, building on Jacobs, is to narrow the focus of such an inquiry to the field of *theological* literature.

Some contemporary philosophers also attempt to delineate a "principle of charity" for their discipline, consisting of tenets that encourage us to, for example, understand a point of view in its strongest form, assume coherence, and attempt to resolve apparent contradictions.[6]

4. Augustine, *On Christian Teaching*, trans. and ed. R. P. H. Green (Oxford: Oxford University Press, 2008), 27.

5. Alan Jacobs, *A Theology of Reading: The Hermeneutics of Love* (Boulder, Co: Westview, 2001), 9–11.

6. George Hunsinger helpfully summarizes some of the philosophical literature on the principle of charity and applies it to the reading of Barth. See George Hunsinger,

While quite helpful, these principles may not be radical enough. The love of neighbor that Jesus enjoins us to practice is a reflection of God's love for us, revealed in Christ's self-offering. This love involves giving oneself to another, intentionally pursuing another's good with no expectation of reciprocation.[7] The specific shape of this neighbor love is spelled out throughout the New Testament through positive and negative examples of what it means and does not mean to love others as ourselves. In what follows, we will examine a small sampling of New Testament passages that deal directly with love, with the aim of discerning potential obstacles to love before applying these observations to the act of reading theology. Specifically, we will look at the obstacles of pride, suspicion, favoritism, and impatience—what I would call the "enemies of love."

Enemy 1: Pride

Love . . . does not boast, it is not proud. (1 Cor. 13:4)

Pride, according to Augustine, is "an appetite for a perverse kind of elevation," a "perverted imitation of God." He adds, "For pride hates a fellowship of equality under God, and wishes to impose its own dominion upon its equals, in place of God's rule. Therefore, it hates the just peace of God."[8] Pride is animated by a devilish desire to be great, and greatness is construed primarily as "greater *than*." Rather than enjoying the fellowship of equals, pride delights in exaltation over others, even God. Pride is opposed to humility. Jonathan Edwards helpfully defines humility as a sense of one's "comparative meanness" when measured against God and fellow creatures.[9] Our lowliness before God is twofold: natural and moral. The first refers

---

Reading Barth with Charity: A Hermeneutical Proposal (Grand Rapids: Baker Academic, 2015), xii–xiv.

7. I have in mind some understanding of *agape* or charity.

8. Augustine, *City of God against the Pagans*, Cambridge Texts in the History of Political Thought, trans. and ed. R. W. Dyson (Cambridge: Cambridge University Press, 2013), 15.13; 19.12.

9. Jonathan Edwards, "Charity and Its Fruits," in *The Works of Jonathan Edwards*, ed. Paul Ramsey (New Haven: Yale University Press, 1989), 8:233–34.

to the recognition that humanity is infinitely below God in natural perfection, or that God is infinitely above us in greatness. The second refers to the appreciation of one's moral vileness in the face of God's infinite holiness. Edwards sums up this form of human meanness: "His natural meanness is his littleness; his moral meanness is his filthiness."[10] Following from our sense of lowliness before God, we can see our meanness with respect to creatures of superior rank and even fellow humans. "He who has a right sense of himself with respect to God," Edwards writes, "*will open his eyes to see himself aright in all respects.*"[11] What this suggests is that humility sharpens our eyesight or even lifts the veil that prevents fallen people from seeing things rightly. Pride, on the other hand, brings a kind of blindness—a blindness to ourselves, others, God, and ultimately all reality.

In "Revelation," Flannery O'Connor tells the story of Mrs. Turpin, a proud white woman from the South.[12] Much of the story takes place in a doctor's waiting room as Mrs. Turpin and her husband, Claud, await his examination. As they wait, she surveys the motley clientele populating the room: the "stylish lady" sitting next to her, who does nothing but flatter her; the ugly college girl reading a textbook, who does nothing but scowl; the white-trashy old woman, mother, and child, adorned in pitiful clothing; the common woman tirelessly chewing gum.

While there, Mrs. Turpin covertly examines people's shoes and determines the social class to which they belong. Mrs. Turpin is the kind of woman "who would occupy herself with the question of who she would have chosen to be if she couldn't have been herself."[13] Given the option between white trash and black, she decides she'd be a "clean respectable Negro woman, herself but black."[14] She sometimes lies awake at night naming and ordering the various classes of people: blacks on the bottom with white trash, then homeowners, then land and homeowners—her class—and then the wealthy. Now,

10. Edwards, "Charity and Its Fruits," 8:235–36.
11. Edwards, "Charity and Its Fruits," 8:235 (emphasis added).
12. Flannery O'Connor, "Revelation," in *Everything That Rises Must Converge* (New York: Penguin, 1983), 405–24.
13. O'Connor, "Revelation," 407.
14. O'Connor, "Revelation," 408.

as she sits in the waiting room, she feels pretty good about herself, especially compared to the less savory characters surrounding her. In her conversations with the only person worthy of her attention—the stylish lady—she cannot help but express her settled views about the classes. But every time she makes a self-exalting or others-disparaging comment, she notices the ugly college girl's angry eyes fixed on her— and she can feel the glare.

Mrs. Turpin engages in a long and haughty discourse about the inadequacies of black people and the follies of white trash, culminating in the exclamation, "If it's one thing I am . . . it's grateful. When I think who all I could have been besides myself and what all I got, a little of everything, and a good disposition besides, I just feel like shouting, 'Thank you, Jesus, for making everything the way it is!' It could have been different!"[15] After enduring this tirade long enough, the ugly girl hurls her textbook at Mrs. Turpin's head, pounces on her, looks her straight in the eyes and whispers, "Go back to hell where you came from, you old wart hog,"[16] and then passes out.

The rest of the story is about Mrs. Turpin, unable to shake those words, trying to make sense of how *she of all people* could be a wart hog from hell—she with such a wonderful disposition. In the end, the words of a maniacal girl prove revelatory; they open Mrs. Turpin's eyes to see herself for who she really is. Pride blinded her from seeing things clearly. Everything was interpreted in light of her perceived superiority. No one could be seen for what they were intrinsically but only for what they were in comparison to her, which was not much. Rather than enjoying the fellowship of equals, as Augustine put it, she delighted in exaltation over others.

One line from O'Connor's story illuminates the influence of pride when it comes to reading. Of Mrs. Turpin, O'Connor writes, "There was nothing you could tell her about people like them that she didn't know already."[17] Pride has a self-satisfied, self-sufficient orientation. Kevin Vanhoozer, speaking of hermeneutical pride, writes, "Pride

15. O'Connor, "Revelation," 415.
16. O'Connor, "Revelation," 416.
17. O'Connor, "Revelation," 413.

neglects the voice of the other in favor of its own."[18] The proud
have no need of others and what they might contribute; they know
everything already. Pride's characteristic disdain for equality has a
corrupting influence on reading. If I already know what I need to
know, I am less likely to listen to other voices; at least I will not listen
attentively, since they are in fact the voices of my inferiors. In terms
of reading theology, this might translate to interpreting things with
a foregone conclusion in mind. We can pigeonhole theologians so
that no amount of reading will change our opinion.

This sin occurs on both ends of the theological spectrum: conservative and liberal theologians refuse to learn from one another
because the other is not seen as an equal. As Vanhoozer rightly
notes, pride is nonpartisan. In the process of reading theology pride-
fully, however, we become delusional and self-deceived, what Jacobs
calls "quixotic readers," because we only see what we want to see.[19]
But humility, pride's archenemy, drives us to properly estimate our
meanness before God and others so that we are able to recognize
our limits and shortcomings, thus becoming open to the influence of
others. "Humility," Vanhoozer writes, "is the virtue that constantly
reminds interpreters that we can get it *wrong*."[20] Peter Abelard,
speaking about how we should humbly approach past theologians,
writes, "Let us not presume to denounce them as liars, or disparage
them as erroneous. . . . Let us believe it is due more to *our* lack of
understanding, than to their failure in writing."[21] Humility prompts
me to recognize that I do not have the market cornered on theological truth, but that I am in constant need of the palliative breeze
of other, diverse voices blowing through my mind.[22] In the end, how

18. Kevin J. Vanhoozer, *Is There a Meaning in This Text? The Bible, the Reader,
and the Morality of Literary Knowledge* (Grand Rapids: Zondervan, 1998), 463.

19. Alan Jacobs, *A Theology of Reading: The Hermeneutics of Love* (Boulder,
CO: Westview, 2001), 91.

20. Vanhoozer, *Is There a Meaning*, 464.

21. Peter Abelard, *"Yes and No": The Complete Translation of Peter Abelard's
"Sic et Non,"* 2nd ed., trans. Priscilla Throop (Charlotte, VT: MedievalMS, 2008),
11 (emphasis added).

22. An image borrowed from C. S. Lewis in his introduction to Athanasius, *On
the Incarnation*, trans. and ed. by a Religious of C.S.M.V. (Crestwood, NY: St. Vladimir's Seminary, 2002), 5.

can we learn from others if we assume we have nothing to learn from them? Pride is the death of learning, but loving humility is a way to life.

Enemy 2: Suspicion

> Love is kind. . . . It keeps no record of wrongs. . . . [It] always trusts, always hopes. (1 Cor. 13:4, 5, 7)

Love is kind and "thinketh no evil," as older translations render it. Love takes the disposition of thinking the best rather than the worst of people. Even when suspicion may be warranted, love does not carry with it the assumption that people cannot be trusted, even those who may have proven untrustworthy in the past. Love keeps no record of wrongs.

Suspicion, an enemy of love, by definition does not think the best of others; rather, it thinketh evil. This is what Edwards refers to as a "censorious spirit," a fruit of uncharity. He contends that "a Christian spirit is contrary to a censorious spirit; or in other words, it is contrary to a disposition uncharitably to judge others."[23] A suspicious person, according to Edwards, thinks evil about others with respect to three areas: their religious state, their qualities, and their actions. Concerning the first, he means that some people show an eagerness to think ill of others. They may treat others as hypocrites or false believers on the basis of slender evidence or may condemn people for the very failings they see in themselves. Most noteworthy, for our purposes, he adds that some people "will condemn others as those who must needs be carnal men for differing from them in opinion in some points which are not fundamental."[24] Such denunciations come easily to the suspicious spirit, for whom "different" translates as "suspect."

Second, a suspicious spirit is blind to the good qualities of others. Edwards writes,

23. Edwards, "Charity and Its Fruits," 8:283.
24. Edwards, "Charity and Its Fruits," 8:284.

Some men are very apt to charge others with ignorance and folly and other contemptible qualities which in no way deserve to be so esteemed by them. Some seem to be very apt to entertain a very low and despicable opinion of others, and so to represent them to others, when a charitable spirit would discern many good things in them, and would freely own them to be persons not to be despised. And some are ready to charge others with those morally ill qualities from which they are free, or at least to charge them with them in a much higher degree than they are really in them.[25]

Suspicion here functions as a prejudice, rendering one incapable of seeing others rightly. It magnifies bad qualities and minimizes the good.

Third, a censorious spirit tends to impute bad motives to others' actions, whether words or deeds. Typically we have no access to the motives driving someone's actions. Yet some of us are quick to assume ill intent and put "bad constructions" (as Edwards calls them) on actions that, as far as any levelheaded person could tell, are good. This disposition is rightly seen by Edwards as "contrary to Christianity."[26]

Love is kind and always trusts (1 Cor. 13:4, 7); it does no harm to its neighbor (Rom. 13:10) and "covers over a multitude of sins" (1 Pet. 4:8). These verses represent an antisuspicion manifesto. It could be said that love is a form of eager credulity, a trusting in another that makes one vulnerable. Calvin interprets the apostle's "always trusts" as referring to a sort of simplicity and kindness in judging things. The result of this kind of trust, according to Calvin, is "that a Christian man will reckon it better to be imposed upon by his own kindness and easy temper than to wrong his brother by an unfriendly suspicion."[27] Love trusts; it assumes the best. It is not crippled by fear, a close correlate of suspicion.

After denouncing faith as inimical to truth and hope as a fundamentally evil delusion, Nietzsche takes aim at love, writing, "Love is a state in which a man sees things most decidedly as they are *not*." For him, Christian love is a grand illusion. It prevents people from

25. Edwards, "Charity and Its Fruits," 8:284–85.
26. Edwards, "Charity and Its Fruits," 8:285–86.
27. John Calvin, *Calvin's Commentaries*, vol. 20, *I and II Corinthians* (repr., Grand Rapids: Baker, 2003), 425.

living rational, self-governed lives and opens one up to greater delusion by inculcating a passivity toward life. "When a man is in love," he writes, "he endures more than at any other time; he submits to anything."[28] While a malformed love may at times result in what Nietzsche highlights, Alan Jacobs takes a different perspective. Speaking of the risks involved in love, Jacobs responds, "Nietzsche's later thought is driven by fear, but above all else *he fears being deceived* in faith, hope, and love—after all, all three states of mind open one to deception—and would rather suffer anything than the humiliation of being fooled."[29]

Jacobs observes that there is space for a healthy suspicion, one bounded by love for one's neighbor, and he calls this "discernment." This kind of discerning suspicion is contrary to Nietzsche's discerning, which, according to Jacobs, "can only suspect and therefore is not discernment at all—since its conclusions are preestablished." True discernment, while aware of the fallen human condition that occasions suspicion, is "prepared to find blessings and cultivate friendships; in short, to receive gifts."[30] The trust that adorns love cannot escape the possibility of deception if it is going to remain truly open to the other and receive whatever gift attends such loving trust.

How might these general observations speak to the reading of theology? Recall that suspicion judges harshly if disagreements exist, has difficulty seeing the good in others, imputes bad motives, and is averse to trust. These traits manifest themselves in a number of ways as we read theology. First, if in one precious area of theology we find ourselves disagreeing with an author, then we sometimes question the genuineness of the author's Christian faith. This was a common gut-level response of my students to the liberation theology I mentioned earlier. We seem to have no category for disagreeing with a key premise or point yet still finding goodness, sincerity, or truth in the proposal.

Second, sometimes suspicion takes the form of concluding prematurely, in fear, that the author wishes to disrupt or undermine

28. Friedrich W. Nietzsche, *The Antichrist*, ed. and trans. H. L. Mencken (New York: Knopf, 1920), 77.
29. Jacobs, *Theology of Reading*, 88 (emphasis added).
30. Jacobs, *Theology of Reading*, 88.

one's faith. We distance ourselves immediately, almost reflexively, by ascribing a label to the theologian, so that ultimately Nietzsche's fear dominates our reading. We are afraid of being deceived, so we mount a preemptive strike against the potential deceiver. But in the process we lose the gift that the other theologian might confer because loving trust is generative while suspicion is degenerative; one opens doors to understanding and thereby growth, while the other closes doors to both. As C. S. Lewis writes, "We can find a book bad only by reading it as if it might, after all, be very good. We must empty our minds and lay ourselves open."[31] He later adds, "The armed and suspicious approach which may save you from being bamboozled by a bad author may also blind and deafen you to the shy and elusive merits—especially if they are unfashionable—of a good one."[32]

Last, an encounter with a new theology or theologian may produce a certain kind of theological xenophobia. New theologians are foreigners; as such they may arouse suspicion. Related to the previous point, we may think that these foreigners and their way of thinking are going to disrupt our way of life, our values, our beliefs. Thus we keep them at arm's length and lose out on the possibility of understanding because we do not want to enter their world. Suspicion, or the lack of sympathetic embrace, makes understanding difficult.

Enemy 3: Favoritism

Love your enemies, do good to those who hate you. (Luke 6:27)

If you really keep the royal law found in Scripture, "Love your neighbor as yourself," you are doing right. But if you show favoritism, you sin and are convicted by the law as lawbreakers. (James 2:8–9)

We are commanded to love our neighbor and to love our enemy. In the story of the Good Samaritan, we see how these commands are often one and the same. The very illustration of neighbor love offered by Jesus signals that our neighbor is everyone, which will

31. C. S. Lewis, *An Experiment in Criticism* (repr., Cambridge: Cambridge University Press, 2012), 116.
32. Lewis, *Experiment in Criticism*, 128.

unfortunately include those we might view as "enemies." This suggests that the kind of love Jesus commands is antithetical to favoritism or "respect of persons" as it used to be called. Commenting on James 2, Calvin makes the point well: "He, then, who says, that a very few, according to his own fancy, ought to be honoured, and others passed by, does not keep the law of God, but yields to the depraved desires of his own heart. God expressly commends to us strangers and enemies, and all, even the most contemptible. To this doctrine the respect of persons is wholly contrary. Hence, rightly does James assert, that respect of persons is inconsistent with love."[33]

Inherent to the kind of respect of persons that James condemns is the desire to earn the approval of a select group. In the present case, the acts performed toward the rich would, in other situations, be demonstrations of love. However, when angled solely toward the respectable, favored, and privileged and away from the unworthy, despised, and marginalized, these acts are a shell of love. In fact, they are antilove, a transgression of the whole law. Neighbor love is not a quid pro quo arrangement; it does not act with the expectation of receiving something in return. This is evident from the Samaritan parable: no return was to be made by the recipient of love. This is also the case in enemy love. In fact, we can expect to receive the opposite from our enemy. Dietrich Bonhoeffer, speaking of enemy love, writes: "This love knows no difference among diverse kinds of enemies, except that the more animosity the enemy has, the more my love is required. No matter whether it is a political or religious enemy, they can all expect only undivided love from Jesus' followers. . . . We should not only bear evil and the evil person passively, not only refuse to answer a blow with a blow, but in sincere love we should be fond of our enemies."[34] It is not distinctly Christian to love those with whom we have natural, religious, or ideological bonds. We are, rather, commanded to embrace those whom we

---

33. John Calvin, *Calvin's Commentaries*, vol. 22, *Hebrews, I Peter, I John, James, II Peter, Jude* (repr., Grand Rapids: Baker, 1999), 305.

34. Dietrich Bonhoeffer, *Discipleship*, ed. Geffrey B. Kelly and John D. Godsey, trans. Barbara Green and Reinhard Krauss, vol. 4 of *Dietrich Bonhoeffer Works* (Minneapolis: Fortress, 2003), 139.

would otherwise have nothing to do with, even those who would undermine and oppose us.[35]

To return to the matter of pursuing the approval of others, it can be said that love pursued for that end is ultimately self-centered. In *An Experiment in Criticism* C. S. Lewis gives a taxonomy of bad—or "unliterary"—ways to read literature. Among these he includes the "status seekers," those who are "entirely dominated by fashion." Such people read only for the sake of making themselves acceptable to certain elites. They read with some enthusiasm the "approved" literature, particularly new, exciting, and controversial works.[36] Yet their reading is a *using* rather than an *enjoying*. The book and its author are important not in their own right but only for some other end, a self-seeking end. That is, self-seekers want to be "in."

We are now better situated to consider at least two ways that favoritism might undermine the charitable reading of theology. First, we tend to give deference to theologians who are in our "camp." We read their work with charity and try to make the most sense of what they are saying. On the other hand, we may treat theologians who are "foreigners" with suspicion (at best) and quick dismissal (at worst). Yet love of neighbor demands that we not just care for our own—like the "sinners" and "publicans" do—but go out of our way to think favorably about our theological "enemies." Second, favoritism can take the form of status seeking even in theological culture. There are always movements, writers, or books that are *en vogue*. The status seeker tends to read those respected theologians, while despising the simple and less celebrated writers. Ralph Waldo Emerson famously remarked, "To be great is to be misunderstood."[37] This statement, *mis*taken a certain way, becomes the mantra of the status seeker. According to this line of reasoning, sometimes the more obscure and easily misunderstood a theologian is, the better. This tendency

35. Bonhoeffer continues, "Jesus does not need to say that people should love their sisters and brothers, their people, their friends. That goes without saying. But by simply acknowledging that and not wasting any further words on it, and, in contrast to all that, commanding only love for enemies, he shows what he means by love and what they are to think about the other sort of love." Bonhoeffer, *Discipleship*, 143.

36. Lewis, *Experiment in Criticism*, 7–8.

37. Ralph Waldo Emerson, *Self-Reliance and Other Essays* (New York: Dover, 1993), 25.

can manifest itself in students rejecting their theological upbringing because, according to some of them, their upbringing is unsophisticated. Yet we can see how Jesus's love command undercuts this kind of approach to reading. Love requires that we treat the supposedly simple and the putatively profound similarly, which becomes easier if we are not seeking something in return for our act of love, such as praise, respect, or status.[38]

Enemy 4: Impatience

Love is patient. . . . It is not easily angered. . . . [It] always perseveres. (1 Cor. 13:4, 5, 7)

Love is long-suffering, enduring many things for the sake of promoting peace and harmony in Christ's church.[39] It often requires that we bear injury willingly and refrain from a defensive and resentful posture. "Forbearance" is the old term and it evokes thoughts of God lovingly and patiently bearing with his difficult people to the point of sending his Son. Patience is not naïveté; it is a bearing with not only *in spite of* sin and offense but also *in light of* them. Speaking of God's patience, Barth writes:

There can be no question of disappointment or self-deception on the part of God with respect to the sincerity, or insincerity, of the human penitence for which He waits in His patience. God is not short-sighted, nor is He subject to any optimistic illusions, when again and again He saves and preserves Israel only to reap continually wild grapes instead of grapes. God does not, then, experience any disillusionment with regard to his people, the many. He knows very well what is our frame. But because He knows it, He has good ground for being patient with us.[40]

38. None of this means that there are not texts to which some favoritism is well deserved, such as those of the great theologians. These texts tend to be treated with greater care and charity. Thus, they are less in need of defense.
    39. Calvin, *I and II Corinthians*, 422.
    40. Karl Barth, *Church Dogmatics* II/1 (London: T&T Clark, 2010), 419. Hereafter *CD* (page numbers are from the older edition, which are noted in the margin of the 2010 edition).

Patience knows the common weakness of the other's frame and, in that light, endures with him. The ground of this patience, for Barth, is Jesus, so that the one who commands love (here expressed as patience) is the very ground for it. Like God in Christ, our endurance is no mere tolerance. Rather, it is teleological, having the ultimate well-being of the other in view. Long-suffering love, then, is not quick-tempered. It is not looking for opportunities to be offended. One is reminded of James's exhortation: "Everyone should be quick to listen, slow to speak and slow to become angry, because human anger does not produce the righteousness that God desires" (James 1:19–20). Rather than being quick to speak and express anger, we are to "hurry up and listen."[41] Sometimes we find ourselves chomping at the bit to vindicate ourselves, and we fail to listen attentively to what others are saying. Philosopher Mikhail Bakhtin observes, "Lovelessness, indifference, will never be able to generate sufficient attention to slow down and linger intently over an object."[42] Love, conversely, demands attentiveness to the details and particularities of others, and this requires being slow to speak. In other words, love is patient, enduring, persevering. The earlier quote from Emerson, when taken in a different way, might be informative. Before saying, "To be great is to be misunderstood," he names several great thinkers who in their own time were misunderstood. "Is it so bad, then, to be misunderstood?" he asks. "Pythagoras was misunderstood, and Socrates, and Jesus, and Luther, and Copernicus, and Galileo, and Newton, and every pure and wise spirit that ever took flesh."[43] One might infer that had people in their day borne with these great men, these people would have recognized and experienced their brilliance. However, the lack of attention, a possible trait of what Emerson calls "little minds," resulted in not receiving the reward that sometimes awaits the patient and long-suffering.

Jacobs connects these insights to reading through the lens of hope. He writes, "The charitable reader offers the gift of constant and loving

41. Craig L. Blomberg and Mariam J. Kamell, *James*, Zondervan Exegetical Commentary on the New Testament (Grand Rapids: Zondervan, 2008), 85.

42. Mikhail Bakhtin, *Toward a Philosophy of the Act*, quoted in Jacobs, *Theology of Reading*, 53.

43. Emerson, *Self-Reliance and Other Essays*, 24–25.

attention—faithfulness—to a story, to a poem, to an argument, in hope that it will be rewarded. But this hope involves neither *demand* nor *expectation*; indeed, if it *demanded* or *expected* it would not be hope."[44] Patience, according to Jacobs, is displayed by attentiveness to what the author is doing, and this attentiveness produces understanding, not to mention other benefits such as pleasure. This practice is not a characteristic of the "unliterary," the impatient users of texts. Lewis remarks:

> The sure mark of an unliterary man is that he considers "I've read it already" to be a conclusive argument against reading a work. We have all known [those] who remembered a novel so dimly that they had to stand for half an hour in the library skimming through it before they were certain they had once read it. But the moment they became certain, they rejected it immediately. It was for them dead, like a burnt-out match, an old railway ticket, or yesterday's paper; they had already used it. Those who read great works, on the other hand, will read the same work ten, twenty or thirty times during the course of their life.[45]

How many of us have been this unliterary reader? We may have read a work for a school assignment but can scarcely remember what the book was about. Part of the problem is that the book was not patiently attended to, possibly because we were reading it for a purpose other than for enjoyment. A charitable reader understands that books, like people, can be easily misunderstood or, at the very least, incompletely understood; thus they require repeated and persistent engagement. Understanding will not likely come to the "one and done" reader nor to the user.

What bearing do patience and impatience, construed in this way, have on reading theology? First, as mentioned earlier, it is not uncommon for students to ask the impatient question: Where is this found in the Bible? What they might have in mind is concern for the writer to "show his work." If biblical exposition or at least parenthetical references are not explicit, then the theology is pronounced "unbiblical." While all Christian theology must engage Scripture in some

44. Jacobs, *Theology of Reading*, 89.
45. Lewis, *Experiment in Criticism*, 2.

manner, theologians do this in different ways—some explicit and others implicit (as we will see in chap. 3). A patient reader is more likely to find a deeper biblical logic in these "unbiblical" theologies because she is willing to wait and attend to the details of what is being said beyond what might be gleaned at first glance.[46] Love is not quick-tempered and prone to rash judgments.

Second, the concern for practical application to "real life" can sometimes short-circuit the pursuit of understanding. Impatience to "get to the point" is the attitude of a user. Lewis likens this false seeker of understanding to a person who plays games, not to enjoy them, but to improve his body through them. The game exists not as a valuable end to be enjoyed but as a means to a more important end. In the process the game itself is lost. Speaking of sports as well as literature, Lewis writes, "To come to the particular game with nothing but a hygienic motive or to the tragedy with nothing but a desire for self-improvement, is not really to play the one or to receive the other. *Both attitudes fix the ultimate intention on oneself.* Both treat as a means something which must, while you play or read it, be accepted for its own sake."[47] While I would certainly say that the practical questions deserve to be asked, a premature focus on the practical value of a theological proposal diverts attention away from understanding to something more self-centered. If we patiently attend to first things (i.e., understanding), we will likely get the second things (i.e., practical application). If we too quickly attend to second things, we are in danger of losing both.[48]

Finally, following Jacobs, it would appear that hope, or some form of expectation, is a characteristic of a charitable and patient reader. This hope involves trusting that the reading of this particular theologian (to whom I may not be favorably disposed) will yield good fruit if I patiently attend to it. At the very least, we aim for a union

---

46. This approach is akin to what experts in art or literary criticism would call "descriptive criticism": the attempt to patiently understand and carefully describe the work under consideration. This act precedes "evaluative criticism," where the reader or observer assesses the merits of the work. See Ralph A. Smith, *The Sense of Art: A Study in Aesthetic Education* (New York: Routledge, 2014), 52.

47. Lewis, *Experiment in Criticism*, 8–9 (emphasis added).

48. This idea is adapted from Lewis's essay titled "First and Second Things." See C. S. Lewis, *First and Second Things: Essays in Theology and Ethics*, ed. Walter Hooper (Glasgow: Collins, 1985), 19–24.

of understanding, though not necessarily agreement. But like most unions of any worth, this will be a hard-fought victory achieved through persevering, slow-tempered love.

Love's Knowledge, or How Would Jesus Read?

Though this book is about learning to read theology both critically and charitably, it should be clear that these are not mutually exclusive activities but rather are complementary. For example, we saw that a patient reader is an attentive reader, and few things are more important to a critical reading than enduring attention to the details. What this suggests is that love can contribute to knowledge, a knowledge that only comes through a form of union with another. This is a deeply Christian notion; it is a variation of faith seeking understanding. It was Anselm who famously prayed, "But I do desire to understand Your truth a little, that truth that my heart believes and loves. For I do not seek to understand so that I may believe; but I believe so that I may understand."[49] Anselm brings belief and love together and then binds them with knowledge. This principle can be said to apply to our knowledge of others, including the works of authors, who are present in their writing, so to speak.[50] Reading charitably is about respecting an author and extending respect to what the author has crafted. Jacobs observes, "One might say, using Cardinal Newman's terms, that without love one may achieve 'notional' assent to some proposition but remain disabled from any 'real' assent to the proposition's truth."[51] Without love one can know the truth of something in the abstract but not by experience or conviction. A depth of knowledge is opened up only to the lover. Hence, love is not a naïveté that reduces the person (as in Nietzsche) but that which expands the person's capacities to see beyond his or her own horizon. As Lewis notes, to expand ourselves, we must empty ourselves.

49. Anselm of Canterbury, *Proslogion*, in *The Major Works*, ed. Brian Davies and G. R. Evans (Oxford: Oxford University Press, 2008), 87.
50. One author calls this the "semantic presence" of the author (specifically, in his case, referring to God and Scripture). See Timothy Ward, *Words of Life: Scripture as the Living and Active Word of God* (Downers Grove, IL: IVP Academic, 2009), 65–66.
51. Jacobs, *Theology of Reading*, 50.

In love we escape from our self into one other. In the moral sphere, every act of justice or charity involves putting ourselves in the other person's place and thus transcending our own competitive particularity. In coming to understand anything we are rejecting the facts as they are for us in favour of the facts as they are. The primary impulse of each is to maintain and aggrandise himself. The secondary impulse is to go out of the self, to correct its provincialism and heal its loneliness. In love, in virtue, in the pursuit of knowledge, and in the reception of the arts, we are doing this. Obviously this process can be described either as an enlargement or as a temporary annihilation of the self. But that is an old paradox; "he that loseth his life shall save it."[52]

To grow in knowledge, we must hold loosely to our knowledge. This gesturing at emptying ourselves, or what theologians call "kenosis," leads to the place we probably should have begun, that is, with Jesus Christ.

After reminding the believers in Philippi to consider the love they share in Christ (Phil. 2:1), the apostle Paul exhorts them to love one another (2:2), doing nothing out of selfishness and everything out of humility (2:3). The attitude they are to embody—the attitude of love—is patterned after Jesus (2:5). The Son who exists as God does not cling to his rights as God (2:6). As Barth puts it, "He did not consider or treat His equality with God as His one exclusive possibility. He did not treat it as a robber does his booty."[53] Rather, he empties himself (kenosis) by taking the form of a servant (2:7), and his humility culminates in his obedient death on the cross for us and for our salvation (2:8). Without losing himself (i.e., his deity), Jesus takes on a form of servanthood for the sake of our well-being. Why is the shape of the Son's self-offering of significance for Christian love in practice? Barth answers, "It serves . . . directly to emphasise the apostolic exhortation to humility, in which each member of the community is to subordinate himself to the other, not seeking his own but things of others. . . . Any 'mind' that is not directed to it [the Son's condescension], however exalted or penetrating it may be, passes by Christ and therefore passes by God, and is therefore an unchristian 'mind.'"[54]

52. Lewis, *Experiment in Criticism*, 138.
53. Barth, *CD* II/1, 516.
54. Barth, *CD* II/1, 517–18.

The pattern of the self-involving, self-offering, self-emptying love of God is the undoing of pride, suspicion, favoritism, and impatience. In the being and act of Jesus Christ, in his taking on himself the form of a servant and dying on the cross, we see the openness, undeserved favor, patience, and humility of God. Paul's exhortation is that we participate in this kind of love and thus show ourselves to be children of God, shining as stars "in a warped and crooked generation" (Phil. 2:15). Christian love is a cruciform movement toward the other in every sphere, even in our reading of theology.

Conclusion: To Read with Intelligent Charity

By emphasizing charity and the openness that attends it, I do not wish to suggest that there is no room for disagreement and critique when engaging theology. As is the case in marriage, love speaks the truth; it does not completely overlook the faults of loved ones. The openness I am advocating is not an unbounded openness. Rather, love is an open and closed door: open to surprises, to correction, to new ideas; closed to falsehood, to incoherence, to harmful ideas. Judgments must inevitably be made regarding the truth of a theological proposal. The aim of this book is to help those who read theology to develop the skills and habits of head and heart necessary for engaging theological texts well, to the end that we would move from merely visceral responses to more-thoughtful ones. It is my hope that by offering these various considerations, readers will be better equipped to read theology critically, charitably, and with joy as the "happy science" it is.

2

Context, Context, Context

The Backstory of Theology

We must acknowledge the fact that all theologies belong
in a particular context.

—Colin Gunton, "Using and Being Used:
Scripture and Systematic Theology"

The drama of Marilynne Robinson's Pulitzer Prize–winning novel, *Gilead*, centers on the relationship between aging minister John Ames and town prodigal Jack (John Ames) Boughton, the son of Ames's best friend, who happens to be his own namesake and godson. In the story we learn of the shame Jack brings on his family when in his college years he impregnated an impoverished young woman and left town shortly after the child was born, abandoning her and leaving no provisions for mother and child. Despite efforts by Jack's family to rescue the child from the squalor in which she lived, the child died of an infection at age three.

Jack has always been a troubled and wayward child, yet he is the most beloved of his father—a fact that particularly irritates Ames, who rues the pain Jack has brought to his best friend. Ames writes to his own son about Jack: "I don't know how one boy could have caused so much disappointment without ever giving anyone any grounds for hope. . . . He is not the eldest or the youngest or the best or the bravest, only the most beloved."[1]

The story gathers steam when Ames receives news that Jack is returning to town after a twenty-year absence. Their first meeting after decades is filled with tension. On one side, Ames is deeply suspicious, and everything Jack does gets under his skin: Jack's greeting, his questions, his interactions with Ames's young wife and child. On the other side, Jack is well aware of Ames's suspicions, even sensitive to them, but he does little to allay them. Ames, now an old man, feels threatened by the presence of the young man, who is about the same age as his wife.

Several meetings ensue, some involving Ames's wife and son, who are clueless about Jack's past and are very excited about having this stranger around. Conversations between Ames and Jack follow a pattern of suspicion, hostility, and (sometimes supposed) provocation. After a long, exasperating discussion regarding predestination in which Ames feels he is being backed into a corner by the younger Boughton, Ames reflects, "I see the error of *assuming* a person is not speaking with you in good faith. . . . But it is hard for me to see good faith in John Ames [Jack] Boughton, and that's a terrible problem."[2] While deeply aware, even ashamed, of his prejudice against Jack, Ames is unable to shake it, nor is he convinced he must shed it entirely. "People," he maintains, "are fairly and appropriately associated with their histories."[3] Ames doubts that Jack has changed in the twenty silent years, leading him to conclude, "I know nothing about those years, and I believe that I would know—if anything had happened that redounded at all to his credit. He doesn't have the look of a man who has made good use of himself, if I am any judge."[4]

Things between godfather and godson change, however, when the former learns of Jack's recent years. After the only chapter break in the book, we learn that Jack is a father again: he has a black wife

1. Marilynne Robinson, *Gilead* (New York: Picador, 2004), 72.
2. Robinson, *Gilead*, 154.
3. Robinson, *Gilead*, 155.
4. Robinson, *Gilead*, 160.

and a son in Memphis, from whom he has been separated unwill-ingly due largely to the segregationist laws of the time. Jack is a flawed man but now not *only* that. He is also a heartbroken man, a man longing for his family. This revelation softens Ames's heart toward Jack. Jack is not merely a calculating, hard-hearted man whose return to town is contrived to cause more heartache to his family. Godfather is now able to see godson with more depth than he previously could. Ames can now see Jack with compassionate eyes, no longer viewing him as a threat. He begins to recognize the good in the young man. He sees himself. Nevertheless, Jack decides that he must leave town without saying good-bye to his father, who is on his deathbed—once again causing pain to the one who loves him so dearly. But this time Ames understands. Jack's return to Gilead and his abrupt departure are largely acts of mercy toward his dying father. He must leave. He must cause no more shame or pain. He is a family man who, though conflicted, seeks to do right and be reconciled to his kin. The story draws to a close with Ames blessing Jack as he boards a bus leaving town.

● ● ● ● ●

Everyone has a story. We cannot profess to know someone well without sufficient knowledge of his or her story. In fact, we easily misunderstand people when we fail to attend sufficiently to the stories that help explain their actions. What Ames discovers is the revela-tory and heart-shaping power of knowing another's story. Although he had prior and fairly accurate knowledge of Jack, not until Ames receives and understands the fuller story does his heart give way and open to the young man in a less defensive way. Put differently, Ames "read" Jack in light of the only context available to him: Jack's past failures. But a new context was revealed—or rather the old context was broadened—so that now Jack could be read in its light.

What the story of John Ames and Jack Boughton highlights is the importance of knowing context for proper interpretation. On this point, Kevin Vanhoozer writes, "Meaning is an affair of context. To understand what people are saying and doing, we need to know some-thing about the circumstances of their speech and action. Context refers to all those factors in a situation that have a bearing on what our words and acts 'count as.'"[5] This insight, which pervades disciplines such as biblical studies, no less applies to the reading of theology. Knowing the context (or backstory) of a theology is indispensable for reading it critically and charitably. As Alister McGrath rightly observes, "Ideas and theories—including Christian doctrines—must be situated historically, prior to their analysis and evaluation. The historical context of the ideas of an individual or community is not merely dispensable background material to understanding those ideas: the evaluation of those ideas cannot proceed on the basis of the questionable assumption that thought is a socially disembodied process dealing with essentially timeless issues."[6]

Indeed, theology is written from within a context and therefore bears certain contextual marks that must be attended to if we are to understand and assess it well. This is not to say that exhaustive knowledge of the background is necessary for any basic understanding, but knowing some of the circumstances surrounding the text will be invaluable in stimulating critical charity and charitable criticism while reading theologies of all stripes.

In what follows, we will explore three "contexts" or contextual dimensions of theology, the knowledge of which helps to facilitate intelligent reading. First, we explore how theology relates to the *historical-cultural context* out of which it emerges. Second, we examine the different ways theology relates to its *ecclesial*, or churchly, context. Finally, we consider the role that possible theological issues and controversies (the *polemical context*) play in the shaping of theology. In briefly exploring these contexts, I want to help students of theology be aware of what is going on "behind the scenes" of a theological text and as a result become better and more charitable readers of theology. I am convinced that a basic (and hopefully increasing) knowledge of these contexts will help sharpen one's hermeneutical vision by providing lenses that bring the many and varied theologies into clearer focus. Before diving into these specific contexts, we begin by zooming out and considering the role of understanding context generally.

5. Kevin J. Vanhoozer, *The Drama of Doctrine: A Canonical-Linguistic Approach to Christian Theology* (Louisville: Westminster John Knox, 2005), 311.

6. Alister E. McGrath, *The Genesis of Doctrine: A Study in the Foundation of Doctrinal Criticism* (Grand Rapids: Eerdmans, 1997), 92.

Three Contextual Dimensions of Theological Reading	
historical-cultural context	Considers what people and events are shaping the theologian's world
ecclesial or churchly context	Considers where and how the theologian worships God
polemical context	Considers the debates and pressing theological issues of the theologian's time

Barriers to Knowing Context

Like every other human action, theology is contextual; it is a decidedly human act that takes place within a particular historical, social, cultural, and ecclesial setting. And just as other human acts can be misinterpreted if read out of context, such is the case with theology. What exactly constitutes a context? Vanhoozer helpfully responds, "That depends; the circumstances relevant to understanding texts can pertain to the author, to the form of literature, to general background knowledge, or to knowledge of specific situations. . . . The context of textual interpretation should be as broad (or as narrow) as it needs to be in order to make sense of the author's communicative act. The relevant circumstances are those that enable us to identify the game board and the game being played."[7]

Vanhoozer observes that several contextual factors are helpful for interpreting texts: an understanding of the author, the text's genre, situations from which the text arose, and more. With respect to theology, the context of interpretation consists of the circumstances and intentions of the theologian and can be as broad as the situation requires. For instance, Adolf von Harnack, a historian of doctrine, identifies several environmental factors shaping the formulation of doctrine, such as the following:

- The need to update the doctrinal tradition of earlier epochs so that it might be better understood
- The needs of the church's worship and organization

7. Kevin J. Vanhoozer, *Is There a Meaning in This Text? The Bible, the Reader, and the Morality of Literary Knowledge* (Grand Rapids: Zondervan, 1998), 251.

- The effort to adjust doctrines to the prevailing opinions
- The political and social circumstances
- The changing moral ideals of life
- The effort to correct different tendencies and contradictions in the church
- The need to reject once for all an erroneous doctrine[8]

Any or all of these factors—whether cultural or ecclesial—help to give rise to a theological proposal, and knowing them aids our understanding of the theology on offer. Now while most may agree with this basic point, two reasonable objections might be raised. First, what if we cannot access any of the background (for whatever reason)? Second, doesn't all this talk about knowing context remove interpretation from the hands of ordinary people and leave it solely to scholars, since it is such a daunting task to unearth all this background information?[9]

In response to the first concern, we must admit that there will be times when background information is limited to us—because time prohibits our ability to research it, we lack the necessary research skills, or there is no reliable record of the relevant social context. When little background information exists, we may still proceed assuming that our setting shares enough in common with the setting of the theologian to make the writing intelligible. Moreover, the text will often contain enough indicators of the historical-cultural situation, latent assumptions, polemical concerns, and genre. Regarding the second question, it can feel overwhelming to strive for the expertise that a historian like Harnack brings. Yet learning about context need not be an all-or-nothing, either-or arrangement: either learn all the relevant context beforehand or do not read theology at all. The goal is not to make engaging theology impossible by raising the bar too high or by forcing readers to become experts. Rather, the basic point is that for the neophyte and the expert alike, a little dose of

8. Adolf von Harnack, *History of Dogma*, trans. Neil Buchanan, vol. 1 (New York: Russell & Russell, 1958), 12.

9. I borrow these common objections to learning backgrounds from Craig S. Keener, *The IVP Bible Background Commentary: New Testament* (Downers Grove, IL: IVP Academic, 1993), 30–31.

context goes a long way. And the more context one can determine, the more sensitive and intelligent the reading will likely be. With these qualifications in mind, let us reflect on the role of our first type of context—the historical-cultural—in reading theology.

Historical Context: Culture

"Authors are, perhaps most fundamentally, historical agents," writes Vanhoozer.[10] Theological texts, as the product of a historical agent, are thus historical, bearing the marks of their time and place. The relevant historical-cultural context includes factors such as

- *Worldview*: the values or outlook of the author, the recipients, and the overall society; the history of thought in that particular culture
- *Societal structures*: racial dynamics, gender relations, educational issues
- *Economic structures*: issues of wealth, poverty, and class
- *Political climate*: types of government, governmental structures, political parties
- *Religious climate*: issues of pluralism, religious practices and rituals, interactions between religions, convictions, and affiliations[11]

The historical-cultural context is what Edward Farley terms the "environment" in which theology arises. He describes an environment as composed of a *background*, a *situation*, and a *location*. Background refers to the general historical conditions in which the author is writing (e.g., nineteenth-century Germany; Europe during the Second World War). Situation describes specific dimensions of a background that affect an individual's life. For example, a black teenager living in a New York ghetto has a different situation than a black teenager living in a California suburb. Location involves

10. Vanhoozer, *Is There a Meaning*, 232.
11. I borrowed from and modified William W. Klein, Craig L. Blomberg, and Robert I. Hubbard Jr., *Introduction to Biblical Interpretation*, rev. ed. (Nashville: Thomas Nelson, 2004), 239.

those aspects of one's situation that bring about one's social or self-identity, such as race, class, ethnicity, and age.[12] Broad and specific contextual factors inform a theological proposal, and any reader of theology must therefore consider them. This is no startling claim. But sociologist Robert Wuthnow observes that great works of art, literature, philosophy, and, I must include, theology always relate enigmatically to their cultural context. He writes, "They draw resources, insights, and inspiration from that environment: they reflect it, speak to it, and make themselves relevant to it. And yet they also remain autonomous enough from their social environment to acquire a broader, even universal and timeless appeal."[13] Thus the crucial issue for the reader involves describing the specific relationship between theology and the various aspects of historical-cultural context.

For example, one might note that Karl Barth's theology developed in twentieth-century Germany and Switzerland and consequently bears the signs of that age: its political uncertainty, its history of philosophical and cultural thought, its modes of argumentation, its use of the German language, and so on. That is, Barth's theology was influenced generally by his surroundings, his background. This is surely informative. Yet we might go further into his liberal theological training, his experience of the First World War and the rise of Nazism, his early ministry as a pastor to lower-class workers, his university teaching posts, and the regnant theological issues of the day (such as the problem of the knowledge of God). This inquiry into Barth's situation would surely yield other and possibly deeper insights into his thought—why Barth said the things he said the way he said them. For instance, it is well known that much of Barth's earlier theological project was a direct response to the theological liberalism of his teachers and their sanctioning of Germany's entrance into war. Reflecting on his break with his teachers, Barth writes:

12. Edward Farley, "Ecclesial Contextual Thinking," in *Shaping a Theological Mind: Theological Context and Methodology*, ed. Darren C. Marks (Aldershot, UK: Ashgate, 2002), 15.
13. Robert Wuthnow, *Communities of Discourse: Ideology and Social Structure in the Reformation, the Enlightenment, and European Socialism* (Cambridge: Harvard University Press, 1993), 3.

One day in early August 1914 stands out in my personal memory as a black day. Ninety-three German intellectuals impressed public opinion by their proclamation in support of the war policy of Wilhelm II [last emperor of Germany] and his counselors. Among those intellectuals I discovered to my horror almost all of my theological teachers whom I had greatly venerated. In despair over what this indicated about the signs of the time I suddenly realized that I could not any longer follow either their ethics and dogmatics or their understanding of the Bible and of history. For me at least, 19th century theology no longer held any future.[14]

For Barth, liberal theology had no future because it was capitulating to the spirit of the age. Its God always sanctioned and approved of the values of sophisticated German society and never challenged them. Talk about God amounted to little more than talk about humanity. In light of this view of God, it is not difficult to see why many of his teachers could support what Barth deemed a disastrous war policy. Whatever was good for society had a divine stamp of approval. However, for Barth, if we are going to speak about God, we must speak of God as one who confronts and disrupts our assumptions rather than confirms them.[15] Knowing Barth's historical-cultural context sheds light on the way he speaks of the revelation of God, for example, as something that can never be presumed or assumed to be present in nature and society; rather it is something given freely by God himself that interrupts our lives.

Historical-cultural contexts can exert both an intentional and an unintentional influence on the theology in question. Theologians sometimes self-consciously allow an aspect of their situation or location to determine the emphases and outlook of the proposal. Farley illustrates this influence of context when he writes, "For example, being a woman or a man will inevitably shape thinking in a certain way. Being a woman or a man may or may not be explicitly attended in a project of thinking. Thus in a program of thinking, context takes on the additional connotation of those strands of background, situation

14. Karl Barth, *The Humanity of God* (Louisville: Westminster John Knox, 1960), 14.

15. See John R. Franke, *Barth for Armchair Theologians* (Louisville: Westminster John Knox, 2006), 28–31.

and location that are attended to, given thematic and criteriological weight."[16] Theologians are also not always aware of (nor intending to make explicit) the influence of their context on their work. This does not exempt their work from being a product of their place and time. In fact, McGrath remarks, "The influence of the past, paradoxically, is at its greatest precisely when it is undetected or unacknowledged— when certain present-day axioms and presuppositions, allegedly self-evident, in fact turn out to represent the crystallized prejudices of an earlier generation."[17] Although McGrath is speaking specifically about the influence of the past on the present, his comments no less apply to historical-cultural context generally. Whether or not a theologian is conscious of it or wants it to be the case, her work will be influenced in some way by her environment.

Wise readers of theology, therefore, must grow through practice in their awareness of the different kinds and degrees of sway a context holds, for dangers lurk on two sides. On the one side is the possibility of *overstating* the role of context (or certain aspects thereof) and thus reading into the theology something that is not there. In doing so one would fail to note the enigmatic character of theology's relation to context (as mentioned earlier). On the other side looms the possibility of *understating* the role of context in a theological proposal, resulting in the failure to see much of what the theologian is specifically addressing, instead filling in the details from our own experience or understanding.[18] Some further examples will help illuminate these dimensions of context.

Example 1: Moltmann and the "Crucified God"

The theological career of Jürgen Moltmann, one of the most influential theologians of the twentieth century, began when he was seventeen years old, having just survived air attacks that decimated his hometown during the Second World War. Fifty thousand people died

---

16. Farley, "Ecclesial Contextual Thinking," 17.
17. McGrath, *Genesis of Doctrine*, 82.
18. See John H. Walton, *Ancient Near Eastern Thought and the Old Testament: Introducing the Conceptual World of the Hebrew Bible* (Grand Rapids: Baker Academic, 2006), 25.

on the last night of the bombing, including Moltmann's best friend. That night he asked his very first theological questions: "Where is God?," "Why am I not dead too?," and "What am I alive for?" The would-be student of physics and mathematics concluded, "These questions are still with me today. To find an answer to them became more important to me than the formula $e = mc^2$."[19] Shortly after these events, he became a prisoner of war for three years. From there he began to study theology, driven by curiosity to answer those initial questions about God. To understand Moltmann's theology, one must know of its beginnings in his exposure to war and human suffering. In the years that followed, Moltmann allied himself closely with those suffering under dictatorships in Eastern Europe, Latin America, and South Korea, and he was deeply moved by the horrors of Auschwitz. In response to these concerns, he wrote *The Crucified God* (1972; English translation 1973), one of his most influential as well as more controversial works. In it he claims:

> There is unwilling suffering, there is accepted suffering and there is the suffering of love. Were God incapable of suffering in any respect, and therefore in an absolute sense, then he would also be incapable of love. If love is the acceptance of the other without regard to one's own well-being, then it contains within itself the possibility of sharing in suffering and freedom to suffer as a result of the otherness of the other. Incapability of suffering in this sense would contradict the fundamental Christian assertion that God is love.[20]

How should someone read this bold assertion, this rejection of the long-standing doctrine of divine impassibility? Whatever we are to do with it, we must recognize what lies at the heart of his concern: *the question of where God is in the midst of human suffering*. This is a theodicy. On the basis of God's action on the cross, Moltmann moves beyond traditional boundaries and categories to try to make

19. Jürgen Moltmann, "A Lived Theology," in *Shaping a Theological Mind*, 87. See also Jürgen Moltmann, *A Broad Place: An Autobiography* (Minneapolis: Fortress, 2009).

20. Jürgen Moltmann, *The Crucified God: The Cross of Christ as the Foundation and Criticism of Christian Theology*, trans. R. A. Wilson and Margaret Kohl, first American ed. (Minneapolis: Fortress, 1974), 230.

a case for a God who does not stand apart from suffering, apathetic to human pain. Rather, the God revealed in the death and resurrection of Jesus is one with us, suffering with us, even as one of us. It is clear that the background and situation in which Moltmann operated influenced his perspective more than just indirectly. Instead, the situation of sufferers worldwide and his own solidarity with them was a central consideration, one that drove (even if it did not determine) his program and affected central Christian teachings, such as the nature of God's attributes. How does knowing Moltmann's historical context shape our reading of his work? By understanding the pressing sociocultural issues, we at the very least can develop sympathy with Moltmann's project—realizing that his chief aim was not to circumvent or destroy traditional Christian teachings—even if many will still part ways with some of his conclusions. If we are to read with critical charity, we must attempt to see and feel the depths of the concerns to appreciate the theological lengths to which one would go to try to address them.

Example 2: Gutiérrez and A Theology of Liberation

In the introduction to his seminal *A Theology of Liberation*, Gustavo Gutiérrez describes his goal:

> This book is an attempt at reflection, based on the gospel and the experiences of men and women committed to the process of liberation in the oppressed and exploited land of Latin America. It is a theological reflection born of the experience of shared efforts to abolish the current unjust situation and to build a different society, freer and more human. My purpose is . . . to reconsider the great themes of the Christian life within this radically changed perspective and with regard to the new questions posed by this commitment. This is the goal of the so-called *theology of liberation*.[21]

Here we have what we might call a strongly self-conscious perspectival theology, where Gutiérrez deliberately adopts the vantage

---

21. Gustavo Gutiérrez, *A Theology of Liberation: History, Politics, and Salvation,* trans. and ed. Caridad Inda and John Eagleson, rev. ed. (Maryknoll, NY: Orbis, 1993), xiii.

point of the poor and marginalized lay Christians of Latin America, among whom he lived and served for much of his life. This approach will feel foreign to many readers, particularly those who have grown up unaware of their power and privilege. In the eyes of a middle-class American Christian, the foreignness of this proposal has at least two dimensions. First, it is written from a poor, Latin American perspective not from a middle-class, white European or American perspective. What we earlier called the situation (e.g., poverty, ghetto life, existence under dictators) and location (e.g., Latin America) of his theology is deliberately foregrounded in a manner not found in many other theologies. Second, Gutiérrez describes theology as a reflection on the lived experience of poor Christians, who have been marginalized by both the elites and the institutional church, rather than merely a reflection on Scripture or tradition.

This approach immediately moves theology from the safe places to the streets, from the head to the hands, so to speak. It explicitly acknowledges a perspective—some might even say a privileged perspective—from which to interpret Scripture (i.e., from that of the poor). It makes no pretense of objectivity but rather advocates a bias toward the poor, with whom God is in solidarity. Given the lens through which the Christian faith is deliberately viewed, certain elements will be more heavily weighted while others are underemphasized (whether rightly or wrongly). For example, when liberation theologians reflect on the Exodus account and prophetic denunciations of injustice, they often stress salvation as "liberation," attempting to foreground the social and political dimensions of sin as they affect the most vulnerable, such that salvation corresponds (or responds) to those dimensions for those people. Gutiérrez writes, "Salvation embraces all persons and the whole person; the liberating action of Christ—made human in this history and not in a history marginal to real human life—is at the heart of the historical current of humanity; the struggle for a just society is in its own right very much a part of salvation history."[22] Liberation is "integral," involving all aspects of human life, individual and social, "spiritual" and historical.

22. Gutiérrez, *Theology of Liberation*, 97.

What, then, is the value of knowing Gutiérrez's context? A key to reading these theologies is to engage them as overt and unapologetic contextual theologies that stress the historical, social, and political rather than the otherworldly dimensions of salvation. If we are unaware of the historical, social, and political situation to which and from which a theology speaks, we may fail to understand why, for example, certain themes are emphasized at the expense of others. We may end up charging the theology with "imbalance" because it fails to attend to the issues we deem central. On a related note, coming to grips with Gutiérrez's context can alert us to the contextual nature of our own theology. No theology is ahistorical. All theology bears the marks of its culture, assumptions, values, and emphases. When we understand that our own theology expresses our context and will therefore display its share of "imbalances," we can sympathetically and charitably read others with whom we may ultimately disagree. But such disagreement must take place only after the other has been properly heard.

Ecclesial Context: Church

As with the historical-cultural setting, every theologian has some relationship to a church or tradition. Stanley Hauerwas writes, "One of the most important questions you can ask theologians is where they go to church."[23] The critical and charitable reader must learn about the theologian's churchly context and its key characteristics and then be aware of the specific relationship between the theologian's work in question and that context.

One sometimes learns of a theologian's ecclesial affiliation through explicit statements, while at other times the reader has to discover this background through research into the theologian's biography. Often, because of limited time and opportunity, the reader must try to discern church background from clues within the text, such as terminology, emphases, and method. Thus to better discern ecclesial influence in a

---

23. Stanley Hauerwas, *Sanctify Them in the Truth: Holiness Exemplified*, 2nd ed. (London: T&T Clark, 2016), 168. Farley writes, "For most theologians the community of faith is never merely distant background. Insofar as it has created identity, it is a facet of the theologian's location, and insofar as it is an actual living institution, it influences the situation of the theologian." Farley, "Ecclesial Contextual Thinking," 17.

theological proposal, one must be armed with at least a basic understanding of the central themes and motifs of the various Christian traditions. While most traditions and churches seek to be well balanced in their overall theological structure, and while diversity exists within traditions, every tradition implicitly or explicitly presents certain elements or particular approaches as central to Christian truth. The following list provides examples of key themes within a few prominent traditions.[24]

Roman Catholic

The *sacraments* or "sacramental economy" are a major focus in Catholic thought. Christ communicates the benefits of his work chiefly through the sacraments, and "the whole liturgical life of the Church revolves around the Eucharistic sacrifice and the sacraments."[25] Much Catholic theological reflection, therefore, centers on the practice of the sacraments and the insights this generates regarding church life and mission. The theme of *authority* is also particularly pervasive in Roman Catholic thought. Whether we are speaking of papal or episcopal authority, the relation of Scripture and Tradition, papal infallibility, or the celebration of the sacraments, a common underlying concern is that of the locus of authority for Christian life and practice.[26]

Lutheran

Justification by faith is the doctrine by which the Lutheran church stands or falls; Luther states, "Upon this article all things depend

24. In what follows I rely heavily on W. David Buschart, *Exploring Protestant Traditions: An Invitation to Theological Hospitality* (Downers Grove, IL: IVP Academic, 2006). In this volume Buschart summarizes Lutheran, Anabaptist, Reformed, Anglican, Baptist, Wesleyan, Dispensational, and Pentecostal traditions and deals with their historical background, theological method, and characteristic themes. I also recommend H. Wayne House's *Charts of Christian Theology and Doctrine* (Grand Rapids: Zondervan, 1991). Though not comprehensive, it is a helpful overview for beginners of a variety of approaches to central areas of Christian teaching. The Doing Theology series by T&T Clark provides more thorough introductions to various traditions, written by and for people within those traditions.

25. US Catholic Church, *Catechism of the Catholic Church: Complete and Updated* (New York: Image, 1995), 315.

26. Adrian Hastings, "Catholicism," in *The Oxford Companion to Christian Thought* (Oxford: Oxford University Press, 2000), 101–2.

which we teach and practice."[27] According to theologian J. A. O. Preus, "The article of justification serves a kind of hermeneutical principle in the light of which we understand all else that God has revealed in Scripture. All theological talk begins and ends with it."[28] While other traditions believe in justification by faith alone, none place it at the gravitational center of theological reflection in the way Lutherans do. For Lutherans, the *theology of the cross* is a fundamental orientation to the theological task and the Christian life. Luther writes, "He deserves to be called a theologian, however, who comprehends the visible and manifest things of God seen through suffering and the cross."[29] The knowledge of God and thus true theology comes through contemplating the crucified Christ, not through the independent contemplation of the cosmos. "He who does not know Christ," Luther contends, "does not know God hidden in suffering."[30] Here we find the Lutheran emphasis on the humanity of Christ and the simultaneous hiddenness and revelation of God found therein.

Reformed

The *sovereignty of God* in creation, providence, and salvation is at the center of Reformed theology. God creates everything by his word, and this implies a strong distinction between Creator and creatures. God governs everyone and everything, directing them to the fulfillment of his free and sovereign will. Moreover, the one who creates and sustains is the only one able to redeem. While his redemption cannot be presumed, God nevertheless works omnipotently to save his people. Corresponding to the emphasis on God's majesty and sovereignty is the emphasis on the *grace of God*. All that is good in this world is a result of the free grace of God, whether we are speaking of what is known as common grace or of saving grace. Highlighting

27. Martin Luther, *Smalcald Articles* II.1, http://bookofconcord.org/smalcald .php#goodworks.

28. J. A. O. Preus III, "Justification by Faith," quoted in Buschart, *Exploring Protestant Traditions*, 48.

29. Martin Luther, *Heidelberg Disputation, 1518*, in *Luther's Works*, ed. Jaroslav Pelikan, vol. 31 (St. Louis: Concordia, 1957), 52.

30. Luther, *Heidelberg Disputation*, 53.

sovereignty and grace results in the summative emphasis on everything being for *God's glory alone.*

Methodist

Prevenient grace, that is, grace that frees the will of sinful humanity to accept or reject Christ, is a characteristic soteriological principle within Wesleyanism. While Methodists follow the Reformed, for instance, in viewing fallen humanity as devoid of the ability to choose God, they consider the restoration of human faculties to be a universal gift to all through the atoning work of Christ, rather than a particular grace given to the elect. Salvation, then, is a real working together of God and humanity, even though God is the initiator and liberator of the will. *Personal holiness* is also a distinctive emphasis in Methodism. The goal of the Christian life is holiness, and for some Christians this may manifest in what Wesleyans call Christian perfection or entire sanctification—a work of God by which believers are freed from sin and perfected in love for God and neighbor. While not entirely neglecting theoretical concerns, Wesleyan theology is chiefly oriented around the *experience* of salvation.

What is the value of knowing these themes? While much more could be said of each tradition, being aware of these themes alerts us to why certain language and concepts are used. Moreover, having even a basic understanding of these themes helps to illuminate the assumptions and reasons for certain emphases in many theological proposals. Theology students must do the work of understanding these various traditional emphases because this helps to explain what might otherwise look like imbalances in some theologies.

How Traditions Are Used

Not only is it profitable to be aware of the theologian's churchly tradition, but it is also helpful to be aware of how she interacts with that tradition within her theological proposal. We can begin to grasp the variety of ways the church influences a theology by exploring two common modern ways of describing a particular theological formulation: *doctrine* (or *dogma*) and *theology*. Doctrine has several meanings, but it can be described as *the accepted teachings of the church or particular church community.* Sometimes the term *dogma* is used, but both terms refer to shared beliefs, the faith of the universal church or of a particular church communion. Theology is often contrasted with doctrine to mean *the particular understanding of an individual who may or may not be volitionally committed to these same ideas.*[31] The distinction is between corporate belief and individual innovation or criticism. The individual theologian, while standing within a tradition or church community, may or may not conform entirely to its doctrines. Put another way, as theologians operate within a tradition, they can speak (1) *from* it, (2) *against* it, and/or (3) *apart* from it.[32]

Regarding the first option (i.e., speaking *from* the tradition), we can describe doctrine or dogma as a boundary for the theologian. Colin Gunton lays out this relationship between dogma (or doctrine) and theology through the metaphor of gardening: "So far as the relations of dogma to theology are concerned, dogma is that which delimits the garden of theology, providing a space in which theologians may play freely and cultivate such plants as are cultivable in the space which is so defined."[33] The theologian is a gardener with only certain plants to cultivate within a limited space, yet he is at liberty to make the garden as useful and beautiful as his skill and the Spirit enable. Speaking from the tradition of the church refers to the idea that the theologian uses the resources afforded him by his tradition, not to challenge it, but to enrich and expand it. Freedom within limits, play within borders—this is one way the theologian is influenced by his church.

Concerning the second option (i.e., speaking *against* the tradition), when Barth famously described *dogmatics* as "the scientific

---

31. According to Alister McGrath, theology "more properly designates the views of individuals, not necessarily within this community or tradition, who seek to explore ideas without any necessary commitment to them." *Genesis of Doctrine,* 10–11. For the entire discussion of these distinctions, see McGrath, *Genesis of Doctrine,* 1–12.

32. Of course this is complicated by the relative weight one places on the doctrines of traditions, such as those found in the Westminster Confession, and ecumenical creeds like Nicaea and Chalcedon. The theologian's freedom, we might say, is far more limited in the case of the latter.

33. Colin E. Gunton, *Intellect and Action: Elucidations on Christian Theology and the Life of Faith* (Edinburgh: T&T Clark, 2001), 1.

self-examination of the Christian Church with respect to the content of its distinctive talk about God," he made space for criticism (or speaking "against") within the theological task.[34] Theologians are not slaves to dogma or church doctrine; they are called to determine if the church's speech about God is in accordance with God's revelation. The third category (i.e., speaking *apart* from the tradition), perhaps that of academic theologians, is the "freest," so to speak. In this case, theologians are not limited by church doctrine or church audience. Rather, they usually operate from within an academic context, and their task is to commend (or not commend) the rationality and coherence of Christian belief to a broader audience. This requires a certain awareness of and responsiveness to Christian truth as well as broader cultural truth claims.[35]

What is the value of being aware of each of these options for theologians' engagement with their church? First, knowing that a theologian is speaking from or against his or her church makes one cognizant of why certain words, concepts, and assumptions are employed rather than others. This knowledge demands that we think alongside the theologian, within his or her framework. In doing so, we recalibrate our expectations of what should be said and how it should be said, which opens us up to reading with sympathy and better understanding. Moreover, this knowledge alerts us to the possibility that the theologian is reaching outside his or her tradition to enrich or correct it (thus further making the case that we need to have a growing knowledge base of Christian traditions and theologians). Second, knowing that theologians may be speaking apart from their church cautions us against overstating the influence of the church on their theology. Theologians may have little concern for the tradition of which they are a part. They may employ concepts and frameworks that are foreign to their tradition. The able reader of theology will have a working knowledge of Christian traditions and seek to develop the skill of discerning the particular ways theologians interact with their church traditions, so as to read with understanding (that is, critically) and charity. To further illuminate how theologians engage

34. Barth, *CD* I/1, 3.
35. What I have outlined here relates to the issue of understanding theological "genres," a topic I address in chap. 4.

the church's tradition, we turn to two brief examples from the theological work of Barth and Bonhoeffer.

Example 1: Barth on the Doctrine of Election

Barth's innovative doctrine of election is a fine example of critically rethinking a doctrine from within the framework of a particular tradition—in this case the Reformed tradition. Readers who seek to understand Barth's position without this knowledge will be prone to either too easily identify with his views or too quickly reject them. Barth positions himself in continuity with those who have dealt with the doctrine responsibly throughout history by outlining three common concerns that have motivated all careful treatments of the doctrine of election: (1) the desire to preserve the freedom of God's grace; (2) the need to safeguard the mystery of God's will; and (3) the wish to expound the righteousness of God in election.[36] All three concerns are united by a common emphasis on the graciousness of grace, and their strength lies in their ability to both humble and exalt humanity.[37] The divine act of grace always precedes human action. Therefore, the elect can boast of nothing save the grace of God. Yet though God is free, God chooses to love in that freedom and thus exalts humanity. While making abundantly clear humankind's limitations, traditional doctrines of election also bestow a dignity and privilege on those to whom God's electing love is directed. An accurate Christian self-understanding begins with a basic understanding of the doctrine of election.

The problem, however, with typically Reformed construals of the doctrine is that they speak of election and reprobation as equal, balanced concepts, rather than placing election above reprobation. According to Barth, election is not "a mixed message of joy and terror, salvation and damnation," where the no of God is as loud as the yes.[38] Instead (and this is central in Barth's treatment) the doctrine of election is at the heart of the gospel. Thus his thesis reads, "The doctrine of election is the sum of the Gospel because of all the words

36. Barth, *CD* II/2, 19–34.
37. Barth, *CD* II/2, 27–28.
38. Barth, *CD* II/2, 13.

that can be said or heard it is the best: that God elects man; that God is for man too the One who loves in freedom."[39]

Rather than being a word of terror and damnation, "it is itself evangel: glad tidings; news which uplifts and comforts and sustains."[40] The doctrine of election is good news, according to Barth, because it heralds a God who in a primal decision determined himself to be for humanity in Jesus Christ.[41] As the "election of grace," it is at once the will and determination of God to be for humanity (election) and the demonstration and overflowing of the love that is constitutive of his being (grace).[42] Divine election is about the love of God; it has as its goal fellowship between God and humankind.[43] It is the sum of the gospel.

The doctrine of election is located within the doctrine of God because it centers on God's election of himself in Jesus Christ.[44] Election is the primal decision in which God determines to be who he is, which involves being the one who loves us in his Son, who is both the electing God and the elected man.[45] Intrinsic to the election of Jesus Christ is a positive turn toward the creature. "In Jesus Christ," Barth contends, "God in His free grace determines Himself for sinful man and sinful man for Himself. He therefore takes upon Himself the rejection of man with all its consequences, and elects man to participation in His own glory."[46]

What results from this Christocentric turn is a reinterpretation of the Calvinistic view of double predestination. Instead of having elect and reprobate individuals determined before the creation of the world, God determines for himself, in Jesus, loss and death and rejection, but for humanity gain and life and election.[47] Barth writes, "The

---

39. Barth, *CD* II/2, 3.
40. Barth, *CD* II/2, 12. Barth acknowledges that the tradition (1) emphasized reprobation for good reason and (2) tried to expound the doctrine positively (for comfort, assurance, etc.). His burden, however, is to make the doctrine a proclamation in which we are to rejoice. Barth, *CD* II/2, 13–16.
41. Barth, *CD* II/2, 6–7.
42. Barth, *CD* II/2, 9–11.
43. Barth, *CD* II/2, 25–26.
44. Barth sees his treatment as unique in that he places election within the doctrine of God, not the doctrine of the works of God. Barth, *CD* II/2, 76.
45. Barth, *CD* II/2, 103.
46. Barth, *CD* II/2, 94.
47. Barth, *CD* II/2, 162–63.

divine predestination that is to be equated with the election of Jesus Christ [is] a double predestination, [is] the primal act of the free love of God in which He chooses for Himself fellowship with man and therefore the endurance of judgment, but for man fellowship with Himself and therefore the glory of His mercy."[48] Consistent with his treatment of election thus far, Barth presents double predestination as itself gospel; it is God's overwhelming yes to humankind in Jesus Christ. Therefore, election, even in its more shadowy aspects, points to the grace and love of God as constitutive not only of *God's* nature and work but of the church's self-understanding and calling.

How is Barth interacting with the tradition, and how does this inform our reading of his work? What we have seen is a significant revision of traditional Reformed accounts of election. Yet Barth's doctrine operates with the same categories (e.g., decrees, double predestination) and places similar stress on God's sovereignty and grace—two particularly Reformed emphases. Knowledge of Barth's ecclesial context helps us discern both the traditional and the peculiar moves he makes and assess them accordingly. In fact, one's acceptance or rejection of Barth's view may be indicative of a reader's prior sympathy or antipathy to the Reformed view.

Example 2: Bonhoeffer and "Religionless Christianity"

Our second example is taken from a contemporary of Barth's, Dietrich Bonhoeffer. Unlike Barth, Bonhoeffer was reared in a Lutheran setting, and his theology reflects this particular influence. Let us briefly examine one of Bonhoeffer's most controversial proposals: "Religionless Christianity."

In one of his letters from prison written to his good friend Eberhard Bethge, Bonhoeffer writes:

> What keeps gnawing at me is the question, what is Christianity, or who is Christ actually for us today? The age when we could tell people that with words—whether with theological or with pious words—is past, as is the age of inwardness and of conscience, and that means the age of religion altogether. We are approaching a completely religionless

48. Barth, *CD* II/2, 197.

age; people as they are now simply cannot be religious anymore. . . .
How can Christ become Lord of the religionless as well? Is there such
a thing as a religionless Christian? If religion is only the garb in which
Christianity is clothed—and this garb has looked very different in
different ages—what then is religionless Christianity?[49]

Bonhoeffer wrestles with the question of what place Christianity
has in a world "come of age," that is, an enlightened world that does
not see its need for God, a world for which weakness cannot be presumed, a world of strong, advanced, and autonomous people. The
time is over when one could assume that people have a felt need for
God. The age of religion is dead. If Christianity is to continue, it must
be interpreted in a nonreligious or "worldly" way. Some writers, such
as John A. T. Robinson, took Bonhoeffer's religionless Christianity as
a call for the secularization of Christianity, a summons to construe
the faith in a way that would be more relevant to modern people.[50]
Secular assumptions and categories of thought were, therefore, necessary for representing Christianity in contemporary society. The
transcendent God of classical Christian theism must be replaced by
one who is more this-worldly and more reflective of the perspectives
common to the modern world. On the surface, Bonhoeffer does seem
to be suggesting something along those lines. However, if we read
closer and in light of his Lutheran framework, we will see that he is
advocating something quite different.

We must first tackle the meaning of the term *religious* to Bonhoeffer. It appears he has a fairly straightforward understanding of the
term. He writes, "It means, in my opinion, to speak metaphysically,
on the one hand, and, on the other hand, individualistically. Neither way is appropriate, either for the biblical message or for people
today."[51] Religion is concerned with an abstract metaphysical concept
of God and with personal salvation. Furthermore, religious people
"speak of God at a point where human knowledge is at an end . . .
or when human strength fails. Actually, it's a deus ex machina that

49. Dietrich Bonhoeffer, *Letters and Papers from Prison*, ed. John W. de Gruchy,
trans. Isabel Best et al., vol. 8 of *Dietrich Bonhoeffer Works* (Minneapolis: Fortress,
2010), 362–63.
50. See John A. T. Robinson, *Honest to God* (London: SCM, 1963).
51. Bonhoeffer, *Letters and Papers from Prison*, 372.

they're always bringing on the scene, either to appear to solve insoluble problems or to provide strength when human powers fail, thus always exploiting human weakness or human limitations."[52] However, once humans regain their strength, God is cast to the periphery until he is needed again. This is what it means to be religious, and Christianity can no longer be cast in that light.

This is where Bonhoeffer's Lutheran background, and particularly its emphasis on the theology of the cross, provides insight for interpreting his "religionless Christianity." Rather than addressing us in our supposed weakness, God comes to us in our strength. I quote Bonhoeffer at length:

> Our coming of age leads us to a truer recognition of our situation before God. God would have us know that we must live as those who manage their lives without God. . . . God consents to be pushed out of the world and onto the cross; God is weak and powerless in the world and in precisely this way, and only so, is at our side and helps us. Matt 8:17 makes it quite clear that Christ helps us not by virtue of his omnipotence but rather by virtue of his weakness and suffering! This is the crucial distinction between Christianity and all religions. Human religiosity directs people in need to the power of God in the world, God as deus ex machina. The Bible directs people toward the powerlessness and suffering of God; only the suffering God can help. . . . [The] world's coming of age, which has cleared the way by eliminating a false notion of God, frees us to see the God of the Bible, who gains ground and power in the world by being powerless. This will probably be the starting point for our "worldly interpretation."[53]

Rather than having a God who is an afterthought, one who meets needs we could not finally meet, the Christian God is at the center of all of life, not by asserting his power over human weakness but by being pushed aside in the weakness of the cross. The true God is to be found in suffering, not elsewhere. And this suffering God—Christ—is

---

52. Bonhoeffer, *Letters and Papers from Prison*, 366. "Deus ex machina" refers to a concept or idea that is introduced to solve a difficult problem, usually in a facile manner. In this case, God is postulated as the simple answer to all of humanity's problems without much thought.

53. Bonhoeffer, *Letters and Papers from Prison*, 479–80.

a God for others. He liberates human society through surrendering to it. What this means for Christians is that their lives are to be patterned after the one who confronts the secular world in its strength, not by seeking power over it nor by retreating from it. Rather, Christians serve others by reducing themselves in the belief that the power to change the world lies in weakness. One commentator concludes, "Religionlessness is not a refutation but a challenge to a Christianity that asks: 'How can Christ become Lord of the religionless as well?'"[54]

What appears to be a sanctioning of modern liberal theology is in fact an exposition of the theology of the cross. God will be seen and truly reign among the secular only when he is seen in his weakness—on the cross. What is the value of knowing Bonhoeffer's ecclesial context? When we understand that the theology of the cross is at heart an attack against religion and theology done apart from the cross at the center, then we can properly understand what Bonhoeffer means by nonreligious Christianity and avoid the error of labeling him a poster child of a secular theological perspective.

Polemical Context: Conflict

Often overlapping with the historical and the ecclesial settings of theology is its polemical context. Controversy is an unavoidable and necessary ingredient in maintaining a vibrant tradition—especially the Christian tradition. Alasdair MacIntyre writes, "Traditions, when vital, embody continuities of conflict."[55] Not very long into a student's introduction to theology, it becomes obvious that much Christian doctrine has been formulated in the furnace of theological conflict. The central issues in the debates often set the parameters and limit the scope of the doctrine's formulation in its original context and in subsequent discussions. The critical and charitable reading of doctrine is fostered when one is attuned to the often polemical nature of theology. Let us explore a few examples.

54. Christian Gremmels, "Afterword," in Bonhoeffer, *Letters and Papers from Prison,* 589.
55. Alasdair MacIntyre, *After Virtue: A Study in Moral Theory,* 2nd ed. (Notre Dame, IN: University of Notre Dame Press, 1984), 222.

Creeds and confessions are attempts to define what is to be believed (*credo*) and confessed in the face of opposing views. The Creed of Nicaea (325) is a wonderful illustration of the shaping influence of conflict. As a response to Arian denials of the equal deity of Jesus and the Father, the council declared both positive statements and anathemas against the opposition. After a brief statement regarding the Father ("We believe in one God the Father All-sovereign, maker of all things visible and invisible"), the creed goes to great lengths to define who Jesus is in relation to the Father:

> And in one Lord, Jesus Christ, the Son of God, begotten of the Father, only-begotten, that is, of the substance of the Father, God of God, Light of Light, true God of true God, begotten not made, of one substance with the Father, through whom all things were made, things in heaven and things on the earth; who for us men and for our salvation came down and was made flesh, and became man, suffered, and rose on the third day, ascended into the heavens, is coming to judge the living and dead.

Following this lengthy and technical description is a brief statement on the Holy Spirit ("And in the Holy Spirit") and a concluding set of condemnations against the Arians:

> And those that say, "There was when he was not,"
> and, "Before he was begotten he was not,"
> and that, "He came into being from what-is-not,"
> or those that allege, that the son of God is
> "Of another substance or essence"
> or "created,"
> or "changeable,"
> or "alterable,"
> these the Catholic and Apostolic Church anathematizes.[56]

It is obvious that the focus on Jesus is purely a response to particular denials by the Arians. The positive statements (that he is "begotten

---

56. The Creed of Nicaea is taken from *Documents of the Christian Church*, ed. Henry Bettenson and Chris Maunder, 3rd ed. (Oxford: Oxford University Press, 1999), 27–28.

not made," that is, he is the uncreated God rather than a created one, and that he is "of one substance" rather than of a different or similar substance) and anathemas (denouncing the idea that he is "created" or "changeable") dominate the creed. This is no "balanced" trinitarian statement, as evidenced by the paltry partial sentence devoted to defining belief in the Holy Spirit.

In the years after the council, other heretical groups arose that explicitly denied the deity of the Spirit. The Tropici held that the Spirit was an angel of highest rank and different in substance from the Father and the Son. Others like Eustathius of Sebaste argued that the Spirit held a middle position between God and other creatures, being neither God nor one of God's creatures.[57]

It fell to theologians and church leaders such as the Cappadocian fathers to define and defend the church's beliefs regarding the nature of the Spirit and thus the Trinity. In the years leading up to the second ecumenical council, Constantinople (381), they carefully defended the full deity of the Spirit. The creed that was produced by this council, which was substantially influenced by these theologians, bore the marks of sustained reflection on the Spirit in light of the conflicts that had arisen. Rather than merely affirming belief in the Holy Spirit, the Nicene-Constantinopolitan Creed states, "And in the Holy Spirit, the Lord and life-giver, Who proceeds from the Father [and the Son], Who is worshiped and glorified together with the Father and Son, Who spoke through the prophets."[58] Without speaking of the Spirit as "of the same substance" as the Father and the Son, this statement tries to make explicit the equality of the Spirit with the Father and the Son by defining the Spirit's eternal mode of origin as "procession" and by advocating that equal honor be given to all persons of the Godhead. Yet one would be correct to suppose that the creed could have said more and said it more forcefully, as we find, for instance, in the Athanasian Creed.[59]

---

57. See the fuller discussion in J. N. D. Kelly, *Early Christian Doctrines*, rev. ed. (Peabody, MA: Prince, 2003), 255–60.

58. Taken from John H. Leith, ed., *Creeds of the Churches: A Reader in Christian Doctrine from the Bible to the Present*, 3rd ed. (Louisville: Westminster John Knox, 1982), 33.

59. This creed says, for example, "Now this is the catholic faith: That we worship one God in trinity and the trinity in unity, neither blending their persons nor dividing

What these episodes in the history of doctrine highlight is not merely that theological conflicts often stimulate the clear articulation of Christian belief. More importantly, these episodes also illustrate that theologians do not often say everything they could or should say on a matter. What they do say is said in ways that would be adequate for the original situation but may not suffice today. Apparent imbalances in articulating arguments, insufficient treatments of subjects, or even silence on certain matters can sometimes be explained by an examination of the conflict from which the theology arose.

This pattern is seen not only in early creedal formulae but also in later confessional statements like the Formula of Concord (1577), as well as the works of individual theologians. Concerning the former, the subtitle to the formula indicates its somewhat limited aims: "A Thorough, Pure, Correct, and Final Repetition and Declaration of Some Articles of the Augsburg Confession about Which, for Some Time, There Has Been Controversy among Some Theologians Who Subscribe to Them, Decided and Settled according to the Analogy of God's Word and the Summary Contents of Our Christian Doctrine."[60] It is clear that this particular confession of faith was chiefly concerned with in-house controversies—among those subscribing to the Lutheran Augsburg Confession (1530)—though it also addressed broader debates regarding the Lord's Supper, the person of Christ, and predestination.[61] Although more could have been said by way of furnishing a complete statement of Lutheran teaching, this statement limits its topics and the arguments therein to the controversies at hand. Its aim is to clarify the decisions made in the earlier confession. In addition, even the substantive *Institutes* of Genevan theologian

their essence. For the person of the Father is a distinct person, the person of the Son is another, and that of the Holy Spirit still another. But the divinity of the Father, Son, and Holy Spirit is one, their glory equal, their majesty coeternal." See "Athanasian Creed," https://www.crcna.org/welcome/beliefs/creeds/athanasian-creed.

60. "The Formula of Concord, Solid Declaration," in *Concordia—The Lutheran Confessions: A Reader's Edition of the Book of Concord*, ed. Paul Timothy McCain et al., 2nd ed. (St. Louis: Concordia, 2006), 503.

61. See Jaroslav Pelikan, *Credo: Historical and Theological Guide to Creeds and Confessions of Faith in the Christian Tradition* (New Haven: Yale University Press, 2003), 199–200, for helpful discussion of the formula and its relation to previous confessions.

Francis Turretin, the great systematizer of Reformed teaching, is a limited work. In his preface, he writes:

> Let no one think that a full and accurate system of theology is delivered here. For this was not indeed the design proposed to me, but only to explain the importance of the principal controversies which lie between us and our adversaries (ancient and modern) and supply to the young the thread of Ariadne, by the help of which they may more easily extricate themselves from their labyrinth.[62]

As the *Institutes* unfolds, it is clear from the form and content of the work that his opponents are primarily the Socinians, Roman Catholics, and Arminians (Remonstrants). Given his limited aim, Turretin justly cautions readers: "Hence if anyone desires more in these pages and calls this a crude and immature foetus, he will have me confessing the same."[63] Understanding context requires not only that we know the historical situation broadly speaking and the conflicts that stimulate theological statements but also that we are attentive to the polemical aims of the writer, as these are often disclosed by the author or by a close reading of the contents covered in the text. When we are alert to these specific aims, we are better able to judge the relative success of the theological proposal; that is, we can determine whether the proposal adequately addresses *its* interlocutors, which is primary, before seeing how it addresses our own concerns. Learning the polemical setting of theology thus fosters patience, a key ingredient in charitable and critical reading.

Conclusion: To Know Another's Story

This chapter began with the claim that knowledge of another's story is essential for properly interpreting the other's actions and that this

---

62. Francis Turretin, *Institutes of Elenctic Theology*, ed. James T. Dennison Jr., trans. George Musgrave Giger, vol. 1 (Phillipsburg, NJ: P&R, 1992), xl. The "thread of Ariadne" refers to the key by which someone may navigate out of a maze or labyrinth. It is based on the Greek myth in which Ariadne gave Theseus a ball of thread that would help him find his way out of the labyrinth after killing the Minotaur.
63. Turretin, *Institutes*, xl.

truth applies to reading theology. To speak of theologies as having stories is simply another way of naming the obvious: that theologies arise from within a context, that they have a background. To be able to interpret a theology properly, we must attend to its historical, ecclesial, and polemical contexts. As Nicholas Wolterstorff notes, "If the Christian is going to engage in that practice of our common humanity which is scholarship, then he is thereby under obligation to honor his fellow participants by understanding as well as he can how they are thinking and where, to put it colloquially, they are 'coming from.'"[64] What Wolterstorff claims is not solely for scholars. Rather, charity demands that the theological student learn where a theology is "coming from"—its contexts. In this chapter, we saw that knowing these various contexts sets the stage for critically charitable reading, yielding at least these seven benefits.

1. We can *avoid overstating the role of context* and thus reading into the theology something that is not there. We can *avoid understating the role of context in a theological proposal*, resulting in the failure to see what the theologian is specifically addressing, instead filling in the details from our own experience or understanding.

2. As we learned from the examples of Moltmann and Gutiérrez, we can *develop sympathy with the sociocultural concerns of the theologian* and from there appreciate the measures he or she takes to address them.

3. When we are aware of the historical, social, political, ecclesial, and polemical situations from which a theology speaks, *we can begin to understand why certain themes are emphasized at the expense of others*. We avoid charging the theology with "imbalance" because it fails to attend to the issues we deem central.

4. *We are also alerted to the fact that our own theology is contextual and not neutral or objective*. This awareness may help to foster charity toward those with whom we may ultimately disagree, for the grounds of our disagreement will not be that the other's theology is too culturally situated.

5. Being aware of central theological themes within Christian traditions and a theologian's ecclesial affiliation *signals why certain*

---

64. Nicholas Wolterstorff, *Inquiring about God: Selected Essays*, vol. 1, ed. Terence Cuneo (Cambridge: Cambridge University Press, 2010), 302.

language, concepts, and assumptions are on display. This knowledge demands that we think from the theologian's perspective or within her framework and adjust our expectations concerning what should be said and how. This practice makes for more sympathetic and knowledgeable readers.

6. As we learned from the examples of Barth and Bonhoeffer, knowledge of their ecclesial contexts helps us *discern both the traditional and the peculiar moves theologians may make and assess those moves appropriately.*

7. Awareness of the polemical setting and the aims of a theology *enables us to better judge its success in its original context so as to temper our judgments with patience.* A particular theological statement may have been adequate in its own context, even if it may not be adequate in today's context. Only after the theology has been properly situated in its context can we determine how effective it is at addressing our own concerns.

While recognizing that limited time and opportunity make it difficult at times to ascertain all these contextual features, we must still aim to know as much of a theology's backstory as possible since our goal is *sympathetic,* critical understanding—a grasp of the text that is neither brash or presumptuous nor naive. Indeed, we must make careful and informed judgments. Yet like John Ames, the character with whom this chapter began, we fail to judge graciously and accurately when we neglect the fuller story.

PART 2

On Reading
CRITICALLY

3

The Bible Tells Me So

Theology and Scripture

Nor indeed is it easy to say what is the meaning of "proving a doctrine from Scripture."

—Benjamin Jowett, "On the Interpretation of Scripture"

When my son was just entering his toddler years, we had a crib-side ritual every night. As I put him to bed I would ask, "What song do you want to sing?" Invariably he responded, "Jesus Loves Me." Often, as our stirring rendition drew to a close, we would repeat the final lines two or three times: "The Bible tells me so, the Bible tells me so, the Bible tells me so." Unbeknown to me (and countless other parents), I was, very early in my child's Christian formation, teaching him a thing or two about theological method. The song makes a profound, even if unsophisticated, theological claim: Jesus loves *me*—he loves a child, a gentile child, an individual child and not merely children generally. This little chorus then asks of each singer, "How do you know Jesus loves you? On what basis are you able to say this?" The response: I know this (and here comes the methodological move) *because* the Bible tells me so. The Bible is a source, *the* final source even, of theological truth. A stretch, maybe, but not too much of one. "Jesus Loves Me" teaches what Christian theologians have almost universally assumed, namely, that a theological claim can be true only insofar as it is drawn from or at least coheres with Scripture. The Bible is the source, norm, fount, or (to use a technical phrase) the *principium cognoscendi* (foundation of knowledge) for all theological reflection. Even where theologians diverge on the relation of Scripture to tradition, reason, or experience, they agree on the centrality and authority of Scripture for Christian theology. Some even contend that to speak of Scripture as authoritative is a truism, a tautology; for to call something Scripture is already to acknowledge its sacredness and special authority in the life of the church.

But the matter quickly gets more complicated when we ask how the Bible's authority is to be exercised and made manifest in any particular theological proposal. What it means for a theology to be (or not be) biblical is not as straightforward as is sometimes thought. Explicit exposition and citation of Scripture do not exhaust the options for establishing a theology's rootedness in Scripture. For example, the Bible may provide a language, a trajectory, or a truth claim (among other things) that will take center stage in a theological account. Recognizing *how* the Bible is being used becomes critical for assessing a doctrine's validity, biblically speaking. It is when we become more aware of this variety that we are better situated to think positively about what criteria will help identify faithful uses of the Bible in theology. This chapter contends that the practice of *sola Scriptura* takes on a variety of forms in theological proposals, and there are a number of factors to consider when assessing the scriptural fidelity of one's theology. To this end, we will first examine the meaning of *sola Scriptura* and its relation to biblical authority in theology. Second, we will address the sundry ways theologians use the Bible. Third, we will survey two perennial issues related to theologians' use of the Bible: proof-texting and the literal sense of Scripture. These explorations will lead us, finally, to several broad principles for assessing a theological proposal's use of Scripture.

What Is the *Sola* of *Sola Scriptura*?

The meaning of the rallying cry "Scripture alone" seems so obvious as to require no further examination. Yet when the watchword is pressed and interpreted in its Reformation and post-Reformation contexts, its meaning is less than transparent. Scripture alone *for* what? Scripture alone *as* what? Certainly the claim concerns the Bible's unique authority in Christian life and doctrine. Yet what is it authoritative as? These become critical questions as we try to assess how "biblical" one's theology is or is not. Anthony Lane quips, "To talk of Scripture *alone* implies the exclusion of rivals."[1] These rivals include tradition, the teaching authority of the church, reason, experience, prophecy, general revelation, and culture. What does *sola Scriptura* claim regarding the Bible's relation to these competitors? Lane provides three less-than-optimal options: it means that Scripture is (1) the only source or resource, (2) the only sufficient source, or (3) the only authority over against its rivals. Let's examine each of these options.

Scripture as the Only Source or Resource

While the distinction between a source and a resource may be difficult to discern and maintain in practice, for our purposes designating something a "source" denotes that it provides indispensable truth or knowledge that contributes significantly to doctrinal formulations.[2] In speaking of something as a theological "resource," I am describing something that functions as a valid aid rather than a fount in constructing theology. For example, a Bible concordance, a resource, is an aid in helping us make expedient use of the Bible, a source. When the issue is framed in terms of truth or knowledge, most would agree that Scripture is a chief, if not *the* chief, source for

---

1. Anthony N. S. Lane, "*Sola Scriptura?* Making Sense of a Post-Reformation Slogan," in *A Pathway into the Holy Scripture*, ed. Philip E. Satterthwaite and David F. Wright (Grand Rapids: Eerdmans, 1994), 298.

2. It might be more a matter of the degree of influence that something has on a theological proposal: sources are at the center, while resources are more peripheral. Lane does note that in practice resources often become sources. Lane, "*Sola Scriptura*," 300–301.

doctrine. Now, does *sola Scriptura* exclude its rivals from functioning as theological aids, resources, or sources?

Take tradition—the wisdom of the Christian church passed down through the ages—as a key example. Although since the Reformation some have unequivocally rejected all appeals to tradition, this was not the standard position among Protestants. To some radicals, traditions are human-made, and an appeal to them is likely to distort the pure truths of Scripture. This is what one author called the "solo Scriptura" rather than a *sola Scriptura* position, and it misses the mark for at least four reasons.[3] First, it is not desirable since it often results in churches repeating the errors of past generations (e.g., rejecting the creeds, then committing a christological heresy). Second, it is not sustainable, since we all approach the Bible with prior understanding of what certain words and concepts mean. This understanding is mediated to us by the two thousand years of Christian reading of the Bible and Christian influence on the world. For instance, we come to a term as basic as "God" with prior conceptions of what the term means—preconceptions likely handed down to us by others. Third, "traditionless" churches invariably establish their own traditions, their own ways of reading and practicing the Bible. Churches that have pastors or teachers are already allowing some "tradition" of interpretation to function as a theological resource—even if that tradition is embodied by only one person. Finally, it should be acknowledged that this was not the position of the Reformers. One need only read Calvin's *Institutes*, with its regular citations of Augustine, its defense of the creeds, and its use of traditional categories for Christology to grasp that for Calvin, as for many leading lights of the Reformation, tradition was an indispensable resource for doing responsible theology.

Let's take reason as a further example. It is not possible to read anything, let alone the Bible, without the use of reason. One must be able to track arguments, detect contradiction, and follow the logic of the various genres in Scripture. Reason also relates to the use of philosophy in theology (which is addressed more fully in chap. 5). If

3. Keith A. Mathison, *The Shape of Sola Scriptura* (Moscow, ID: Canon, 2001).

philosophy is broadly defined as wisdom drawn from human reason and rational observation of the created order with no direct appeals to divine revelation, then surely it can be an aid if it points to the truth. Augustine rightly commends: "Any statements by those who are called philosophers . . . which happen to be true and consistent with our faith should not cause alarm, but be claimed for our own use, as it were from owners who have no right to them."[4] The Reformers, in line with Augustine, made use of philosophy when it helped the cause of truth. They were cautious, yes, but never denied the role of reason in theological formulation. Similar comments can be made regarding experience, general revelation, and other supposed rivals. The *sola Scriptura* position does not deny their value as theological resources. But how about as sources?

When we ask if something can be a theological source, we are asking if it provides truth that contributes to the theological enterprise. If we consider general revelation, it can be said that something apart from Scripture provides knowledge of God. The heavens declare God's glory, pouring forth knowledge (Ps. 19); indeed, all of creation speaks of God's invisible attributes and divine nature (Rom. 1). Creation declares God's wonderful wisdom, Calvin writes, even to "the most untutored and ignorant persons, so that they cannot open their eyes without being compelled to witness them." If this knowledge is available to the untrained who merely observe the world with their naked eye, certainly the principled study of the created order can contribute to our understanding of God and his work of creation. Calvin adds, "To be sure, there is a need of art and of more exacting toil in order to investigate the motion of the stars, to determine their assigned stations, to measure their intervals, to note their properties. As God's providence shows itself more explicitly when one observes these, so the mind must rise to a somewhat higher level to look upon his glory."[5] We come to know God's ways as we observe what he has made. The Westminster Confession puts the matter this way:

4. Augustine, *On Christian Teaching*, trans. and ed. R. P. H. Green (Oxford: Oxford University Press, 2008), 64.

5. John Calvin, *Calvin: Institutes of the Christian Religion*, ed. John T. McNeill; trans. Ford Lewis Battles (Louisville: Westminster John Knox, 1960), I.5.2.

The whole counsel of God concerning all things necessary for His own glory, man's salvation, faith and life, is either expressly set down in Scripture, or by good and necessary consequence may be deduced from Scripture: unto which nothing at any time is to be added, whether by new revelations of the Spirit, or traditions of men. Nevertheless, we acknowledge the inward illumination of the Spirit of God to be necessary for the saving understanding of such things as are revealed in the Word: and that there are some circumstances concerning the worship of God, and government of the Church, common to human actions and societies, which are to be ordered by the light of nature, and Christian prudence, according to the general rules of the Word, which are always to be observed.[6]

Thus while the Bible may be the primary source for theologians, general revelation is also a source of knowledge for them. Scripture alone cannot, therefore, mean "the only source." But can it mean that it is the only *sufficient* source?

Scripture as the Only Sufficient *Source*

Theologian B. B. Warfield, speaking on the matter of sources, compares the "sources" in the science of astronomy to those of theology. He first admits that there can be a theology without Scripture, a natural theology, one gained by observing nature, history, and the human person. Similarly, there can be an "astronomy of nature," a natural astronomy, so to speak, where persons in their natural state and with their naked eyes observe the stars, the moon, and other wonders of outer space. Then Warfield exclaims, "But what is this astronomy of nature to the astronomy that has become possible through the wonderful appliances of our observations? The Word of God is to theology as, but vastly more than, these instruments are to astronomy."[7] As powerful telescopes, not to mention satellites and other technology unavailable in Warfield's day, have taken astronomy to new heights, so the Bible revolutionizes the study of theology. Warfield concludes:

6. "Westminster Confession of Faith," http://www.reformed.org/documents/wcf _with_proofs/.

7. B. B. Warfield, *Studies in Theology*, vol. 9 of *The Works of Benjamin B. Warfield* (Grand Rapids: Baker, 2003), 63.

What would be thought of the deluded man, who, discarding the new methods of research, should insist on acquiring all the astronomy which he would admit, from the unaided observation of his own myopic and astigmatic eyes? Much more deluded is he who, neglecting the instruments of God's Word written, would confine his admissions of theological truth to what he could discover from the broken lights that play upon external nature, and the faint gleams of a dying or even a slowly reviving light, which arise in his own sinful soul. Ah, no! The telescope first made a real science of astronomy possible: and the Scriptures form the *only sufficing* source of theology.[8]

By describing Scripture as "the *only sufficing* source," he provides an expression of the principle of *sola Scriptura*, of the primacy of Scripture in some regard. Yet in referring to Scripture in this way, he implies that there are indeed other sources, even if those sources are not up to the task of strongly grounding theology. There are other sources for doctrine, but the Bible is the only sufficient one. Is Warfield correct? Is Scripture the only sufficient source of theology, and is this the meaning of *sola Scriptura*?

A way to address the question is to consider what some have called "the rule of faith." In the early centuries of the church, various heterodox sects arose claiming to know the meaning of Scripture and therefore what is true for the Christian faith. The orthodox appealed to this "rule"—a summary of the central teachings of Scripture—as a way of discerning who did or did not have a correct understanding of Scripture. It became clear to the early church that there were some who accepted the same Scriptures and based their views on Scripture alone, yet they ended up having deviant understandings of Christ or the Trinity, for example. The "rule" and subsequent creedal statements provide the interpretive key to Scripture. It is what Timothy Ward describes as "a *necessary* tool to ensure that the fundamental teaching of Scripture was constantly upheld in the ongoing task of interpreting the Bible."[9] By speaking of the "rule" as necessary, he is not undermining the foundational and central role of Scripture,

8. Warfield, *Studies in Theology*, 63 (emphasis added).
9. Timothy Ward, *Words of Life: Scripture as the Living and Active Word of God* (Downers Grove, IL: IVP Academic, 2009), 143 (emphasis added).

but he is suggesting that Scripture's sufficiency must be qualified. Rather than playing a merely auxiliary role, creeds or the rule play an authoritative role alongside Scripture in forming doctrine.

Furthermore, Protestant traditions that affirm *sola Scriptura* differ regarding the extent of Scripture's sufficiency. Some, like Anglicans, give the doctrine a more limited focus. According to the Thirty-Nine Articles (an Anglican document), "Holy Scripture containeth all things necessary to salvation: so that whatsoever is not read therein, nor may be proved thereby, is not to be required of any man, that it should be believed as an article of the Faith, or be thought requisite or necessary to salvation."[10] In this view, Scripture is sufficient for matters of faith and salvation alone. Others broaden the reach of the doctrine of sufficiency. For example, the Second Helvetic Confession (a Reformed document) states, "We judge, therefore, that from these Scriptures are to be derived true wisdom and godliness, the reformation and government of churches; as also instruction in all duties of piety; and, to be short, the confirmation of doctrines, and the rejection of all errors."[11] The sufficiency of Scripture extends to the governance of the church. However, the Westminster Confession, as we saw above, takes a circumspect middle course by limiting sufficiency to "all things necessary for His own glory, man's salvation, faith and life," and these must be "either expressly set down in Scripture, or by good and necessary consequence may be deduced from Scripture." While all three examples agree on Scripture's sufficiency in relation to salvation, they disagree (in various degrees) about the doctrine's reach. Yet it is those matters beyond faith and salvation that are often most pressing and most contentious. *Sola Scriptura* cannot be limited to the sufficiency of Scripture for salvation—something to which even Catholics assent—since the principle is also meant to address issues beyond just salvation over against groups like the Catholic Church. If *sola Scriptura* simply means that Scripture is sufficient for matters of salvation, as a rallying cry it is not saying very much.

10. Philip Schaff, *Creeds of Christendom*, rev. ed. (Grand Rapids: Baker, 1966), 1:489.

11. "Historic Church Documents," http://www.reformed.org/documents/index.html.

Finally, and related, Protestant traditions disagree on how to relate *sola Scriptura* to the principle of sufficiency. One could adopt any of the following three positions:

1. We should only believe and practice what is explicitly taught in Scripture.
2. We may believe and practice what is not contrary to Scripture.
3. We may believe and practice that which can be deduced from Scripture.[12]

The first view, held by many Puritans, is difficult to maintain since much of what relates to church life and practice is not explicitly taught in Scripture. If *sola Scriptura* means sufficiency in this sense, then its reach is quite limited. The second view, held by Anglicans and Lutherans, restrains Scripture's sufficiency by acknowledging its limits and allowing for freedom to formulate beliefs and practices not contrary to Scripture but not necessarily taught therein. The third view, as seen in the Westminster Confession, broadens Scripture's reach while not compromising its sufficiency. Therefore, we can see that groups holding to *sola Scriptura* construe Scripture's sufficiency differently. If the Reformers and post-Reformation writers were in agreement on the principle of *sola Scriptura* but were at odds regarding Scripture's sufficiency and its outworking, it appears unlikely that the sufficiency of Scripture is what this universal Protestant affirmation means.

Scripture as the Ultimate Authority

It is best to understand *sola Scriptura* in relation to the question of authority, rather than in terms of sources or sufficiency (though they are related). In this light, the question before us is whether *sola Scriptura* denotes that the Bible is the sole authority over all things pertaining to God. Immediately we have to deny that this is the meaning of *sola Scriptura* since for every writer reason also plays an authoritative role. A contradictory set of statements, for example, will have to pass through the scrutiny of reason. Moreover, as we discussed

---

12. G. R. Evans, Alister E. McGrath, and Allan D. Galloway, *The Science of Theology* (Basingstoke, UK: Marshall Pickering, 1986), 135.

above, tradition also plays an authoritative role in circumscribing possible interpretations of Scripture. In fact, Scripture's authority is preserved by appeal to creeds since these external authorities prevent misreadings of the Bible. As it is, the Bible stands in the company of other authorities, even if we deem them lesser ones.

It is best to view *sola Scriptura* as designating that Scripture is the *final* or *ultimate* authority for all teaching and practice in the church. Scripture is the supreme norm or standard by which all things are judged. The Westminster Confession, for example, says: "The supreme judge by which all controversies of religion are to be determined, and all decrees of councils, opinions of ancient writers, doctrines of men, and private spirits, are to be examined, and in whose sentence we are to rest, can be no other but the Holy Spirit speaking in the Scripture."[13]

Put in traditional language, Scripture is the *norma normans non normata*, that is, the norming norm that is itself not normed (or the ruling authority that is itself not ruled). *Sola Scriptura* is the assertion that the Bible is the supreme norm over tradition, church, experience, visions, miracles, and any other perceived or real religious authorities. Yet framing the matter solely in terms of "final" or "ultimate" judge can appear to place Scripture as an after-the-fact authority, only judging what has already been formulated apart from its decisive influence. However, as the Belgic Confession rightly affirms: "We receive all these books and these only as holy and canonical, for the regulating, founding, and establishing of our faith."[14] Thus it is preferable to say that Scripture is the final authority on the front *and* the back end, both as foundation and as judge. Alister McGrath sums up the matter well:

> The primary source for Christian doctrine is thus scripture, in that it is scripture which mediates Jesus of Nazareth to us. Scripture is the manger in which Christ is laid (Luther). . . . Christian communities of faith orientate and identify themselves with reference to authoritative

13. "Westminster Confession of Faith," http://www.reformed.org/documents/wcf _with_proofs/.
14. "Belgic Confession," https://www.crcna.org/welcome/beliefs/confessions /belgic-confession.

sources which are either identical with, or derived from, scripture. A church which accepts the authority of the creeds does so on account of a belief that they correctly express what is contained in scripture. Scripture, whether approached directly or through a filter of creeds and traditions, is regarded as constituting the foundational documents of the Christian church.[15]

Sola Scriptura means that all doctrine is answerable to the Word as its rule.

While this belief is held by most Protestants (and some Roman Catholics) regarding Scripture's authority, matters get complicated rather quickly when we examine how the authority of Scripture is expressed or experienced in actual theologies. Affirming *sola Scriptura* is one thing; applying it is another. Let's turn our attention to the more complicated issue of living out this Reformation principle.

On the Many Uses of Scripture

In a seminal study on the use of the Bible in modern theology, David Kelsey observes that theologians not only use Scripture in a variety of ways, but they also give pride of place to different aspects of Scripture.[16] One needs to sort through these variations and their attendant complications in order to develop a range of categories for evaluating whether a theology is "biblical." We begin with a survey of some of Kelsey's main insights, as an aid toward establishing principles for assessing theologies.

Early in Kelsey's *Proving Doctrine*, he presents seven case studies meant to highlight the different aspects of Scripture used by theologians and the different ways these aspects are used to authorize theological proposals. Each case study examines one of seven modern Protestant theologians: B. B. Warfield, Hans-Werner Bartsch, G. E. Wright, Karl Barth, L. S. Thornton, Rudolf Bultmann, and

15. Alister E. McGrath, *The Genesis of Doctrine: A Study in the Foundation of Doctrinal Criticism* (Grand Rapids: Eerdmans, 1997), 55.

16. David H. Kelsey, *Proving Doctrine: The Uses of Scripture in Modern Theology* (Harrisburg, PA: Trinity Press International, 1999).

Paul Tillich. Kelsey asks two questions of each theologian that are pertinent to our discussion:

1. What aspect of Scripture is taken to be authoritative?
2. How is the Scripture that is cited brought to bear on theological proposals so as to authorize them?[17]

Though not providing a comprehensive survey of possible responses to either question, Kelsey helpfully illuminates some of the various ways these two questions could be answered. Let us begin with the first.

The Authoritative Aspects of Scripture

What aspect of Scripture is taken to be authoritative? This seems a straightforward question. However, Kelsey exposes the fact that the answers to this question differ depending on the person answering it, as can be demonstrated by examining the work of the theologians Kelsey interrogates. The first theologian, Warfield, appeals to the *doctrines* Scripture teaches as that which is authoritative in a theological proposal. For example, as Warfield constructs his doctrine of the Bible's inspiration, he appeals to 2 Timothy 3:16 and its claim that all of Scripture is "God-breathed." What matters for Warfield is that "inspiration"—that the Bible is the product of divine action—is explicitly taught or asserted by Scripture itself. Similar appeals are made to 2 Peter 1:19–21 and John 10:34. The former asserts, according to Warfield, that all Scripture (here described as "prophecy") is the result of God using human instruments for the purpose of giving Scripture. In the latter passage, Jesus grants a psalm the same authority as legal material, and by implication all of Scripture is given authority as having come from God. Taken together, these passages give us a biblical doctrine of inspiration.[18]

For the second theologian, Hans-Werner Bartsch, it is *biblical concepts* that are authoritative in theology. In what Kelsey calls "biblical concept theology," theologians like Bartsch aim to isolate and define one or another distinctively biblical concept over against nonbiblical

17. Kelsey, *Proving Doctrine*, 2–3.
18. Kelsey, *Proving Doctrine*, 18–21.

(i.e., "Greek") concepts. These concepts then serve as the basis for Christian thought and action today. As an example, in one paper Bartsch contends that reconciliation in the New Testament is better captured by the concept of "peace" than that of "salvation." He traces the historical roots of the term in the Old Testament concept of "shalom" and then argues that "peace" carries with it all the connotations and connections of shalom, including covenant with all its implications. Peace is a technical concept that carries with it layers of rich meaning on which to build a theology of reconciliation. For both Warfield and Bartsch, the authoritative aspect of Scripture is its *content*—as either inspired doctrines or distinct concepts.[19]

The next two theologians, G. E. Wright and Karl Barth, hold that what is authoritative in Scripture is its *narrative* rather than its didactic aspect. However, they construe narrative in different ways. For Wright, narrative is a recital of key historical events, events in which God acted on behalf of God's people. What is foundational is his contention that "God is . . . known by what he has done." Accordingly, the Bible is neither the Word of God nor a collection of doctrines but rather a witness to and recital of God's acts in history.[20] The narrative is the foundation of ideas, not vice versa. Thus when this view of Scripture's authority is put to work on the doctrine of God, for instance, it looks something like this: God acts toward Israel in election and redemption; this leads to a proclamation of what God has done (a *kerygma*); then comes reflection about the nature of God (that God is a gracious Lord).[21] The point here is that narrative—understood as recital—is taken to be the basic starting point and foundation for theological formulation.

For Barth, narrative is also the authoritative feature of Scripture. But rather than focusing on Scripture's narratives as the recital of the historical acts of God, he views them as "identity descriptions." What the Bible's narratives do is make the central character—Jesus Christ— come alive in a way that propositions cannot. Narratives, to use Kelsey's term, *render* an agent or character; they bring us into an encounter with Christ. For example, in Barth's discussion of the person of Christ,

19. Kelsey, *Proving Doctrine*, 24–28.
20. Kelsey, *Proving Doctrine*, 32–33.
21. Kelsey, *Proving Doctrine*, 33–36.

he insists that Jesus's humanity be understood in terms of his story, his history, rather than in metaphysical terms like "nature." In fact, Jesus's whole life—incarnation, ministry, crucifixion, resurrection, and ascension—makes known his will and intention, even his "being." Note that it is not inferences from the narratives but the narratives themselves that bring us face-to-face with God in Christ. The subsequent task of theology is to reflect on Christ and everything in relation to him, but only after his identity is adequately described through engagement with his life history. Therefore, Scripture as narrative only *indirectly* authorizes theological proposals, in opposition to the three examples given above, in which Scripture *directly* bears on theology.[22]

The final three writers share a conviction about Scripture, namely, that it is "authoritative insofar as it expresses the occurrence of a revelatory and saving event in the past and occasions its occurrence for someone in the present."[23] The Bible is a collection of expressions that evoke a certain response or experience from its readers that connects them to the original experience of revelation. Thornton holds that it is the collection of *images* in Scripture that bears authoritatively on a theological proposal. Theology must be attentive to the relationships between images like "Son of Man," "six days," "Messiah," and "suffering," for they put us in touch with the mystery they symbolize. Tillich, along similar lines, sees *religious symbols* (such as stories of the incarnation or the resurrection or the general picture of Jesus as the Christ) as uniquely authoritative because they "*express* the occurrence and content of the original revelation in Jesus as the Christ, and they *occasion* dependent revelatory events having precisely the same content as the original one."[24] These symbols must be conceptualized (i.e., articulate their relation to one another and the whole), explained (i.e., show their relation to that to which they point), and criticized (i.e., show how some symbols are better expressions of original revelation than others).[25] Bultmann, finally, holds that it is Scripture's "kerygmatic statements" (words of personal address, promise, and God's acceptance) and "theological statements" (statements that

22. Kelsey, *Proving Doctrine*, 39–48.
23. Kelsey, *Proving Doctrine*, 83.
24. Kelsey, *Proving Doctrine*, 66.
25. Kelsey, *Proving Doctrine*, 66–69.

express the writers' acknowledgment of God's acknowledgment of them) that are authoritative. The former evokes self-understanding (or faith), while the latter is the normative expression of this self-understanding. Therefore, while both bear on theology, the theological statements are directly, rather than indirectly, authoritative.

The point of all this is that theologians, while acknowledging in some way the authority of Scripture, have different views of what the Bible is fundamentally and, therefore, what aspect of it is authoritative. In assessing theologies, one must at least be aware of these underlying issues.

The Authorizing Use of Scripture

Not only do theologians highlight particular aspects of Scripture; they use them in different ways to authorize their proposals. To "authorize" is to state in some fashion what makes a proposal plausible or true.[26] What are the various ways that theologians use the Bible to authorize their theology?

Most theological arguments follow a familiar pattern with a typical set of premises. Arguments consist of a thesis or claim (C) derived from various sources or data (D).[27] Our move from D to C must be justified by a reason or warrant (W), which itself must be justified by backing (B). Given the elements used to justify C, the concluding claim may need to be preceded by a qualifier (Q) and left open for rebuttal (R) if conditions for rebuttal are established. A simplified example from Warfield's proposal will illustrate the basic structure of arguments.[28]

The data (D) for Warfield's proposal on the nature of Scripture is drawn directly from passages in Scripture that convey doctrinal content about "inspiration." The conclusion (C) is in some sense

---

26. I draw on David Clark's definition: "The process of giving epistemic weight, of ascribing divine authority, of providing appropriate warrant, to the deliverances of theology." David K. Clark, *To Know and Love God: Method for Theology*, Foundations of Evangelical Theology (Wheaton: Crossway, 2003), 87–88.

27. I draw from John M. Frame's helpful summary and analysis in his "The Uses of Scripture in Recent Theology: A Review Article," *Westminster Journal of Theology* 39, no. 2 (1977): 328–53.

28. Kelsey, *Proving Doctrine*, 141. See for example B. B. Warfield, "Inspiration," *The Works of Benjamin B. Warfield* (Grand Rapids: Baker, 2003), 1:77–112.

Figure 3.1

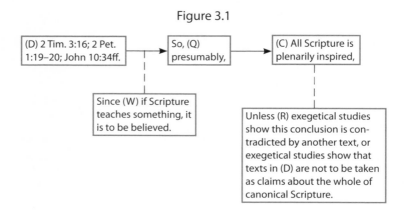

taken directly from the passages themselves. The warrant (W) for this move from D to C is self-evident, given Warfield's terms and what Scripture is by definition. The only way the conclusion (C) can be rebutted (R) in this type of theology is to call into question the data (D) used to support it. This mode of moving from Scripture is quite common in premodern forms of theology.

A second, more complicated example drawn from Tillich's work will move us closer to the point Kelsey is trying to make.[29]

The data (D) of Tillich's proposal regarding how the "power of new being" is mediated to humanity (C) is taken from an analysis of the New Testament's depiction of Jesus. We move from data to claim only by establishing a warrant (W), which is a generalization of how religious symbols function in religious discourse and life. Its backing (B) is primarily drawn from a phenomenology of religious experience, but it is also drawn from Scripture's account of the disciples' encounter with Jesus. Without concerning ourselves with the details of Tillich's theology, notice that Scripture "enters" his proposal at two points: D and B. It provides the picture of Jesus Christ (D) and the paradigmatic instance of religious experience found in the disciples' encounter with Jesus (B). For Kelsey, not only is it possible for Scripture to enter at these two points in a proposal; it may enter at any point in an argument—as D, W, B, Q, R, and/or C—to authorize

29. Kelsey, *Proving Doctrine*, 130. See Paul Tillich, *Systematic Theology*, vol. 2, *Existence and the Christ* (Chicago: University of Chicago Press, 1975).

Figure 3.2

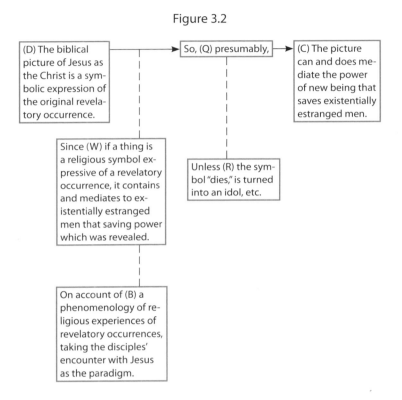

a proposal.[30] Knowing this—as well as different aspects of Scripture that theologians emphasize—should make us more cautious in our assessments of whether a thesis or claim is "biblical" or "based on Scripture." Intelligent reading requires that we ask not merely if a theology "begins" with Scripture (which is a valid but insufficient question) but also how the proposal is rooted in Scripture.

From Scripture to Theology: Two Perennial Issues

Thus far we have clarified the meaning of *sola Scriptura*, a term that refers to the Bible not as the only source but as the final or ultimate

---

30. While I do not think Kelsey demonstrates this well with examples, his main point is reasonable.

authority in all doctrinal matters. We also observed that Scripture exercises its authority in diverse ways in theological formulations. Our concern in this section is to move from clarification and complication to positive principles for doctrinal assessment through an exploration of two perennial issues one encounters when considering how theologians move from the Bible to theology: the problem of proof-texting and the centrality of the literal sense. Following this discussion, the final section will offer principles to guide our assessment of the biblical character of theologies.

The Perils and Promise of Proof-Texting

As a venerable professor at my school used to remark, "Nothing scares New Testament professors more than a theology professor carrying his Greek New Testament." If you have been exposed to biblical studies or theology for even a short time, you will quickly learn that proof-texting is a bad thing. Theologians who proof-text are sometimes charged with being irresponsible with Scripture or with trying to force Scripture into the confines of their airtight system of theology. How many of us have heard the dictum "A text without a context is a pretext for a proof-text"? Proof-texts can be defined as "parenthetical references or footnote/endnote references to biblical passages that undergird some doctrinal claim made, whether in a dogmatics textbook, a catechism, or a confession of faith."[31] What could be wrong with references to the Bible undergirding theological claims? Why does proof-texting have such a negative reputation? These are important questions regarding the biblical nature of theology.

At least three charges are often brought against proof-texting. First, proof-texts do not honor the specific historical or literary contexts of biblical texts. Second, proof-texts often mistake biblical language for doctrinal language, and vice versa, without sensitivity to the complexities of moving from biblical to dogmatic language and categories. Proof-texting can lead to reading our own theology into the biblical text. Finally, proof-texts are shaped more by the history of doctrine than by their interaction with biblical history. We

---

31. R. Michael Allen and Scott R. Swain, "In Defense of Proof-Texting," *Journal of the Evangelical Theological Society* 54, no. 3 (2011): 589.

can become blinded by, for example, the controversies of the past, so that we interpret passages from the Bible chiefly in light of those controversies rather than in light of their immediate context.[32] The case against theological proof-texting appears strong.

Michael Allen and Scott Swain respond by conceding that theologians commit two types of sins with respect to their engagement with Scripture, what they call sins of omission and sins of commission. The first type concerns the lack of serious exegetical work done by major contemporary theologians. While many of these theologians are sensitive to Scripture, consistent and sustained interaction with it is uncommon. The second set of sins, the sins of commission, involves the misuse of Scripture by theologians. Some theologians in this group have a naive understanding of how we move from biblical concepts to doctrinal ones, so that certain theologians end up rejecting traditional doctrines if they cannot find a particular term or concept in a few key verses (or proof-texts) in Scripture.[33] Others in this group misuse Scripture by assuming that one theological position is more justified than another if it can amass more proof-texts than the other. Both misuses betray a naïveté about how the Bible relates to theological formulation. Thus those who employ proof-texting have been guilty of some of the charges leveled against the practice. But is there a more positive way to construe and engage in the practice of proof-texting?

A more charitable account of proof-texting begins with recognizing that authors of the Bible employ proof-texting; thus, the Bible itself is open to many of the charges brought against theologians. Yet many scholars acknowledge that to understand citations of, for example, Old Testament passages in the New Testament, we need a certain sensitivity to the assumptions undergirding the author's citations of Scripture. Allen and Swain write, "If we are to appreciate the way Scripture uses Scripture to prove a doctrinal point, then we

32. Allen and Swain, "In Defense of Proof-Texting," 590–94.

33. Allen and Swain cite Wayne Grudem's rejection of the eternal generation of the Son as a prime example of this tendency. Grudem rejects the doctrine because the Greek term found in each of the key verses (John 1:14, 18; 3:16, etc.) cannot, according to current research, mean "only begotten." Therefore, the notion of eternal begottenness must be foreign to Scripture. See Allen and Swain, "In Defense of Proof-Texting," 595–96.

must appreciate the larger hermeneutical frameworks within which citations are employed, the original (historical and literary) contexts within which proof-texts are found, and we must also possess a certain canonical sensitivity to how biblical motifs and themes unfold in the history of redemption, and, perhaps most importantly, how Christ is understood to be the climax of that unfolding historical development."[34]

Similarly, when we examine proof-texts used in theologians' arguments, we must be sensitive to "the underlying hermeneutical rationale and the broader exegetical context which determined that particular usage."[35] In other words, much is happening beneath the surface when a proof-text is offered. What is going on under the surface of some proof-texting by theologians? Richard Muller points out that many theologians of the past spent long periods of their careers as exegetes and considered the study of Scripture to be essential preparation for the theologian.[36] Speaking of Calvin's *Institutes*, Muller writes, "The *Institutes* must not be read instead of the commentaries, but with them: the commentaries and the *Institutes* together provide, in what Calvin thought to be a better arrangement of materials, what one would find in the commentaries of other writers. Indeed, if one wishes to ascertain the biblical basis of Calvin's topical discussions and disputations, one *must* read the commentaries."[37]

Often when theologians like Calvin "proof-text," they are referring back to the extensive exegesis found in their commentaries or other exegetical works. Even in cases where theologians are not exegetes, they often assume a tradition of established exegesis, to which they only sometimes explicitly refer. Thus when they use proof-texts, they are appealing to the established results of more extensive exegesis on the particular passage in view. Allen and Swain helpfully point out that proof-texts are not the theologian's way of circumventing

---

34. Allen and Swain, "In Defense of Proof-Texting," 597.

35. Allen and Swain, "In Defense of Proof-Texting," 598.

36. Richard A. Muller, *Post-Reformation Reformed Dogmatics*, vol. 2, *Holy Scripture: The Cognitive Foundation of Theology*, 2nd ed. (Grand Rapids: Baker Academic, 2003), 509.

37. Richard A. Muller, *The Unaccommodated Calvin: Studies in the Foundation of a Theological Tradition* (New York: Oxford University Press, 2000), 108. See also Allen and Swain, "In Defense of Proof-Texting," 600–602.

the need to carefully engage the Scriptures. Rather, they represent the need to know the Scriptures deeply and broadly, so as to fully understand the roots of the doctrine under consideration. They conclude, "Understanding the way in which doctrines develop out of and beyond the explicit statements in biblical texts is crucial for grasping the kind of claim made when one gives a proof text: it does not necessarily suggest that the doctrine as stated can be found there, but it does claim that the doctrine is rooted there in principle, when viewed in its larger canonical lens and when its implications are fully teased out."[38]

The lesson for the reader of theology is to not jump to the conclusion that a theologian using proof-texts is "not doing any exegesis" or "doesn't care about the Bible" and so on. Rather, the charitable and properly critical reader will seek to find the deeper biblical logic underlying the employment of particular proof-texts. Proof-texts are not entirely problematic. In fact, they may be shorthand for the right relationship between the Bible and theology.

The Literal Sense: Where Doctrine Is Found

Our discussions of *sola Scriptura*, the Bible's authority, and proof-texting all point to a central issue surrounding how one moves from Scripture to theology: interpretation. The Bible, *as interpreted*, exercises authority in the body of Christ. The church has a rich history of discussions about how to interpret the Bible for doctrinal and practical use by the faithful. An important aspect of these discussions concerns the question of whether Scripture has multiple senses and, if so, which senses are normative for doctrine and practice. Let us consider these multiple senses of Scripture before asking about their doctrinal use.

In the patristic period, the senses of Scripture were broadly divided into two categories, literal and spiritual/mystical. As time went on, and particularly in the medieval period, the spiritual senses were subdivided into three categories, usually allegorical, anagogical, and tropological. The meaning of each is captured in a familiar couplet (followed by its translation):

38. Allen and Swain, "In Defense of Proof-Texting," 602–3.

Litera gesta docet,
quid credas allegoria,
Moralis quid agas,
quo tendas anagogia.

(The letter teaches facts/events,
allegory—what you believe,
Moral—what you do,
anagogy—where you are bound.)[39]

The literal sense, also known as the historical, verbal, or autho-
rial sense, refers to the historical reality to which the words point.[40]
The allegorical sense refers to what must be believed by Christians.
The tropological is the moral sense of Scripture and refers to things
concerning Christian conduct. Finally, the anagogical sense refers to
the eschatological significance of the text. For example, Jerusalem
according to the literal sense is the city of the Jebusites or Jews, but
it is also the church (allegorically), the law or the dwelling place of
God in the soul (tropologically), and the heavenly city (anagogically).[41]
Because Scripture has God as its primary author, it is replete with
wisdom and edification for his people, and these are found in the
spiritual senses of Scripture. How are these spiritual senses related
to the literal, and what does that have to do with doctrine?

Many premodern or precritical interpreters would hold that the
other senses of Scripture must be founded on the literal meaning of
Scripture. What did Reformation and post-Reformation theologians
mean by the literal sense? According to Turretin, who provides a helpful
extended explanation, the literal sense is twofold: *simple* or *compound.*
By "simple" the former refers to when words point to one thing, as
in precepts, doctrines, or histories. These words may be straightforward (or "proper") or figurative, but they have a simple referent. The

39. Nicholas of Lyra, quoted in Francis Turretin, *Institutes of Elenctic Theology*,
vol. 1, *First through Tenth Topics*, ed. James T. Dennison Jr., trans. George Musgrave
Giger (Phillipsburg, NJ: P&R, 1992), 149.
40. Kathryn Greene-McCreight, "Literal Sense," in *Dictionary for Theological
Interpretation of the Bible* (Grand Rapids: Baker Academic, 2005), 455.
41. Greene-McCreight, "Literal Sense," 455. See also J. Todd Billings, *The Word
of God for the People of God: An Entryway to the Theological Interpretation of
Scripture* (Grand Rapids: Eerdmans, 2010), 170–71.

"compound" sense consists of prophecies, which contain both type and antitype, so that the full meaning of the prophecy is not known until type and antitype are joined. Thus the literal sense accounts for the full scope of Scripture—both Testaments—and situates the meaning of a text in light of its canonical placement and function (and ultimately in light of Christ). It is more robust than a literalistic reading of the Bible that does not consider figures, types, symbols, and so forth. As Turretin writes, "The literal sense is not so much that which is derived from proper words and not figurative . . . but that which is intended by the Holy Spirit and is expressed in words either proper or figurative."[42] In agreement with writers like Aquinas, the literal sense is ultimately that which is intended by the Author of Scripture. That being the case, there is only one divinely intended sense to Scripture, and it serves as the foundation for the other senses.

Turretin then makes a distinction between Scripture's senses and its *application*. He categorizes the three spiritual senses as applications of the literal sense in the form of instruction and correction.[43] How does this relate to moving from the Bible to theology? What Turretin proposes, in line with Aquinas and the Reformation tradition, is that doctrine (instruction in the faith) must be rooted in the literal sense of Scripture, not in the other senses.[44] Yet this literal sense, as we have seen, is not what some writers would call the "plain" or "commonsense" meaning of a passage. Such claims often amount to little more than a reductionist view of the literal sense that ignores the various forms of speech found in Scripture. Thus theologians at their best do the hard work of discerning the manifold literal sense of Scripture as they employ it in their theology. What this means is that the reader of theology must be attuned to the literal sense, with its images, metaphors, types, antitypes, and allegories, in order to offer informed and sympathetic assessments of whether theologians are theologizing biblically. The final section on principles for evaluating doctrine develops this point more fully.

42. Turretin, *Institutes*, 1:150.
43. Turretin, *Institutes*, 1:150–51.
44. However, allegory found in Scripture itself is taken up into the literal sense and, therefore, is authoritative in church life. Turretin, *Institutes*, 1:151; cf. Muller, *Post-Reformation Reformed Dogmatics*, 2:479.

Is It Biblical? Principles for Assessing Doctrine

Drawing on these observations and clarifications, I propose seven principles or considerations for asking whether a theology is "biblical." This is not a step-by-step guide, a foolproof method, or an exhaustive catalog of all things needed for assessing doctrine. Rather, these are guiding principles that are helpful in making judgments. Moreover, while few can assess all these things at all times, over time they become more intuitive as one reads more theology and becomes increasingly familiar with Scripture.

1. *What is Scripture?* It is not enough to ask whether a theologian has a "high view of Scripture." However we understand that phrase, a high view does not necessarily lead to a proper use.[45] Our discussion of Kelsey raised the more pressing issue of how theologians construe Scripture, or what aspect of Scripture is in fact authoritative for them. This is a critical matter to settle before assessing a person's theology. Is Scripture chiefly doctrine, narrative, history, expressions of religious experience, or symbols and images? How a theologian answers that question will shape what he does with the Bible. If the Bible is essentially a collection of evocative symbols, its particularities may function chiefly as illustrations of, rather than grounding for, a particular belief. If Scripture is conceived as narrative, details may be downplayed as long as the main storyline is rendered. If Scripture is a variegated collection of doctrines or beliefs, one focuses on propositional statements (and literature) and can simply draw a straight line from biblical statements to contemporary belief.

Vanhoozer helpfully points out that many of these conceptions of Scripture are not in fact wrong, only incomplete; but, in their extreme form, they can lead to a certain theological pathology. Vanhoozer divides theologians into four categories (or quadrants as in fig. 3.3 below). The first category consists of those who emphasize biblical propositions and view them as timeless truths to be systematized by the theologian. This view is correct to acknowledge the Bible as containing divine truths. The dark side, however, is that it sometimes

---

45. This distinction is drawn in Kevin J. Vanhoozer, "Scripture and Theology: On 'Proving' Doctrine Biblically," in *The Routledge Companion to the Practice of Christian Theology*, ed. Mike Higton and Jim Fodor (New York: Routledge, 2015), 142.

Figure 3.3

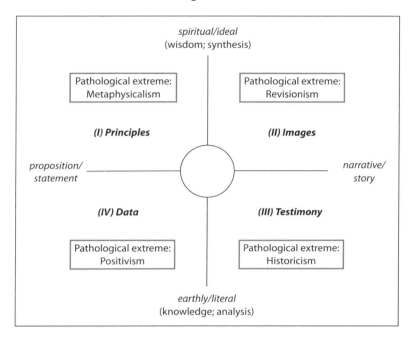

allows extrabiblical philosophies to govern the biblical truths. The second group views Scripture primarily in terms of images that express and lead people to experience the significance of Jesus Christ. This view is correct to emphasize the power of images to transform rather than just inform. The danger is that this view can sometimes disconnect the image from its canonical context and use it in an extrabiblical context, thus distorting it. The third group focuses on the Bible as historical narrative that bears witness to God's acts in the world. While this group is right to see Scripture as a historical narrative finding its climax in Christ, history may be treated naturalistically rather than providentially or redemptively. The final group also focuses on propositions as forms of empirical data rather than as timeless truths. Again, the focus on verbal communication from God is correct. However, in the extreme this view can take the "discrete packets" of data in isolation from the broad narrative of Scripture and from modern biblical scholarship. Each of these perspectives is illustrated in figure 3.3.[46]

The theologian must be attuned to all aspects of Scripture, not just one. The reader of theology needs to discern which aspect of Scripture is being appealed to and preliminarily assess the theology on those terms. Then she must ask if the appeal to just one dimension of Scripture is sufficient or not.

2. *Exegetical directness.* Barth, speaking to a group of students about the theological task, famously said, "Take now my last piece of advice: Exegesis, exegesis, and once more, exegesis! If I have become a dogmatician, it is because I long before endeavored to carry on exegesis."[47] Despite the complexities, discussed earlier, of how theologians authorize their proposals and the inadequacy of asking the question about where a theology "begins," we must still own that the theology is ever answerable to Scripture. Barth observes that the fundamental task of theological study is to "inquire *directly*" into what the Old Testament and the New Testament have to say to the world, the church, and the individual believer.[48] A strong theological proposal has some sort of directness to its engagement with Scripture: it will be energized by rich interaction with the Bible, or the theologian will provide evidence of the groundwork for the proposal. John Frame is correct in saying that to call their theology "biblical," theologians must show where their idea is rooted in Scripture. Frame goes on to say that either principles or specific texts may be employed, so long as a general principle can be demonstrated by a specific text. A theological claim, then, "always boils down in the final analysis to citations of particular texts." So, though we ought to be cautious about the dangers of proof-texting, "proof texts have played a large role in the history of Protestant thought."[49]

46. Diagram and discussion are taken from Vanhoozer, "Scripture and Theology," 149–51.
47. Karl Barth, *Das Evangelium in der Gegenwart*, Theologische Existenz heute 25 (1935), quoted in Richard E. Burnett, *Karl Barth's Theological Exegesis: The Hermeneutical Principles of the Römerbrief Period* (Grand Rapids: Eerdmans, 2004), 30.
48. Karl Barth, *Evangelical Theology: An Introduction* (Grand Rapids: Eerdmans, 1979), 174–75.
49. John M. Frame, *The Doctrine of the Word of God* (Phillipsburg, NJ: P&R, 2010), 574.

As readers, we need to be able to see how a proposal takes its direction from Scripture. Proof-texting is one way this direction is made evident; extensive exegesis is another. There is a moment of truth in standard characterizations of the relationship between exegesis and systematic theology, wherein exegesis leads to biblical theology, which leads to systematic theology (through the guiding hand of historical theology), which finally leads to practical theology.[50] *In principle*, theologies must all be sourced by careful exegesis, even if the theology began with a question or insight from outside Scripture. This is all the more the case with matters at the center of the life and teaching of the church. While I qualify these comments later, the point here is that we need not be reticent to hold theologies accountable to Scripture. The strength and plausibility of every formulation are tied to how much they directly engage with the Bible.

3. *Exegetical excellence.* While exegetical directness is valuable, it is only valuable if the exegesis is done well. Clark Pinnock describes this as "exegetical excellence," namely, that biblical citations used in support of theological claims must be "apt, intelligent, and discerning."[51] Exegetical excellence involves, at the very least, an adherence to the basic rules taught in any introductory course on biblical interpretation, such as attentiveness to contexts and genres. Indeed, theologians can sometimes treat all texts as if they were created equal, rather than taking care to handle them in light of their unique features as poetry, narrative, sermon, law, and so forth.

Exegetical care can also manifest itself as engagement with what one might call the "contemporary consensus," that is, the view taken by the majority of respected and reasonable modern biblical scholars (I would expand the consensus to involve precritical exegetes as well). When such a consensus is not forthcoming, theologians should adopt the "differentiated consensus" of exegetes, or what they may very broadly agree

50. See, for example, D. A. Carson, "Systematic Theology and Biblical Theology," in *New Dictionary of Biblical Theology: Exploring the Unity and Diversity of Scripture*, ed. Brian S. Rosner et al. (Leicester, UK: Inter-Varsity; Downers Grove, IL: InterVarsity, 2000), 102; Nancey C. Murphy, *Reasoning and Rhetoric in Religion* (Valley Forge, PA: Trinity Press International, 1994), 197–98.

51. Clark H. Pinnock, "How I Use the Bible in Doing Theology," in *The Use of the Bible in Theology: Evangelical Options*, ed. Robert K. Johnston (Eugene, OR: Wipf and Stock, 1997), 22.

on.[52] While it is possible that a theologian's reading of Scripture could be better than an expert exegete, this is less likely to be the case. Thus exegetical excellence requires care in one's personal engagement with Scripture, and this may involve deference (*not* unthinking servitude) to the best in biblical scholarship. The question for the reader of theology is, How does this proposal display exegetical excellence?

4. *Attentiveness to the whole canon*. The fittingness of a theologian's use of Scripture, exegesis, and application is tied to his sensitivity to the text's placement within the canon and its relation to other texts throughout Scripture. This principle assumes the unity of Scripture—a complex unity with diversity, but a unity nonetheless. Scripture is, as one writer puts it, "the discourse of the Holy Spirit, the discourse therefore of *one single speaker*, despite the plurality of their human authors."[53] Therefore, what is said in one part of the canon relates to and illuminates in some way what is said elsewhere in the canon. This canonical attentiveness can assume many forms. One simple way to express what I mean by attentiveness to the canon is what Gerald O'Collins and Daniel Kendall call the principle of "biblical convergence." This principle requires that theologians allow the broadest and most diverse portions of Scripture, rather than one solitary verse, to bear on the theological issue in view. The convergence or agreement of the varied biblical witness regarding a particular proposal serves to strengthen that proposal.[54]

Richard Lints provides a helpful model of this principle that is attuned to three "horizons"—or interpretive contexts—at work in biblical texts: the *textual*, the *epochal*, and the *canonical*. The textual horizon refers to the immediate context of the book or passage. Biblical passages are interpreted in light of the textual horizon when the theologian pays attention to the author, genre, immediate literary context, grammar, metaphor, imagery, and history—the basic tools of exegesis mentioned above. The epochal horizon refers to the context

52. Gerald O'Collins and Daniel Kendall, *The Bible for Theology: Ten Principles for the Theological Use of Scripture* (New York: Paulist Press, 1997), 25–27.

53. David S. Yeago, "The Bible," in *Knowing the Triune God: The Work of the Spirit in the Practices of the Church*, ed. James J. Buckley and David S. Yeago (Grand Rapids: Eerdmans, 2001), 70.

54. O'Collins and Kendall, *Bible for Theology*, 24–25.

of the period (or epoch) of revelation in which the book or passage rests. This horizon is attentive to the fact that God's revelation is progressive; it takes form through different epochs.

Each epoch is "distinguished by the different ways in which God has revealed himself and in which his people have understood him."[55] Pre-fall and post-fall, pre-flood and post-flood, pre-Abraham and post-Abraham, pre-Mosaic law and post-Mosaic law, preexilic and postexilic, pre-Christ and post-Christ, preresurrection and post-resurrection: these are all examples of different epochs in Scripture, many of which Scripture itself identifies. Every passage must be understood in light of its place in that particular epoch—the horizon of partial fulfillment, we might say—in redemptive and revelatory history. Is a particular theme especially important in one epoch more than in another? Is God's covenant functioning uniquely in one period versus another? These are the kinds of questions that must be asked of any text. Finally, the canonical horizon refers to the context of all of God's revelation in Scripture. Every passage of Scripture must be read in light of the fulfillment of God's plans in Christ and the church.

Consequently, we understand that the Old Testament is forward looking, like a promise awaiting its fulfillment.[56] At the same time, the New Testament sheds light on the meaning of the Old Testament, sometimes illuminating things the original authors did not perceive. The biblical texts employed in theology must be informed by all three horizons of interpretation. One benefit of this approach, Lints points out, is that the epochal and canonical horizons highlight which issues are important in a text and which are not, considering what the rest of Scripture does with the issue. Theologians will be less likely to fall prey to asking questions of Scripture that it is not asking.[57] The basic point of this principle is that the understanding and use of any particular Scripture text should be informed in some way by the whole of Scripture.[58]

---

55. Richard Lints, *The Fabric of Theology: A Prolegomenon to Evangelical Theology* (Eugene, OR: Wipf and Stock, 1999), 300–301.

56. Lints, *Fabric of Theology*, 301–8.

57. Lints, *Fabric of Theology*, 294.

58. This point is somewhat akin, but not identical, to what theologians have traditionally called the analogy of faith (*analogia fidei*): "The use of a general sense of the meaning of Scripture, constructed from the clear or unambiguous loci, as the

5. *Metathemes and metanarratives.* Directly related to the concern for canonical awareness is the question of how a theology handles or squares with Scripture's major themes and narratives, such as creation, covenant, law, atonement, love, mercy, wisdom, life, idolatry and sin, salvation, the exodus from Egypt, the exile, and the death and resurrection of Jesus.[59] The quality of a theology can be gauged by how well it incorporates these themes and major narrative strands. For example, the problem of suffering cannot be handled in a Christian manner without reference to the death and resurrection of Jesus. The work of Christ cannot sufficiently be addressed without some reference to the atonement theology of the Old Testament, such as the Day of Atonement or the various other sacrifices described in Leviticus. Can a doctrine of the Eucharist ignore the Passover? Can a theological anthropology ignore sin, idolatry, covenant, or even the accounts of Israel's exile?

These themes and narratives must significantly shape Christian theology. If they are sidestepped, the theology on offer—though creative or "constructive"—is inadequate from a Christian perspective. Jowett remarks, "The truth is, that in seeking to prove our own opinions out of Scripture, we are constantly falling into the common fallacy of opening our eyes to one class of facts and closing them to another. The favorite verses shine like stars, while the rest of the page is thrown into the shade."[60] Ongoing attention to the major themes and narratives of Scripture, wedded to an overarching canonical awareness, helps to mitigate Jowett's concern.

6. *Indirect grounding.* With all our talk about exegetical directness, it would be easy to assume that all good theology must have a straightforward "proof" in Scripture, and that doctrines can be read right off the page of Scripture without further ado. However, it has been a long-standing principle that doctrines can be stated in Scripture either explicitly or implicitly. In fact, Turretin contends that *all* teachings of the faith contained in Scripture are implicit, rather

---

basis for interpreting unclear or ambiguous texts." Richard A. Muller, *Dictionary of Latin and Greek Theological Terms: Drawn Principally from Protestant Scholastic Theology* (Grand Rapids: Baker, 1989), 33.

59. This principle is drawn from O'Collins and Kendall, *Bible for Theology*, 27–28.

60. Benjamin Jowett, "On the Interpretation of Scripture," in *Essays and Reviews* (London: J. W. Parker, 1860), 366.

than on the surface of the text.[61] The indirect or implicit grounding of theology takes a few forms. One form brings us back to the
Westminster Confession, which states, "The whole counsel of God
concerning all things necessary for His own glory, man's salvation,
faith and life, is either expressly set down in Scripture, or *by good and
necessary consequence may be deduced from Scripture*" (emphasis
added). The notion of consequence refers to the idea that certain
things are true if one follows the logic and overall direction of Scripture, even if the truth is not stated explicitly. Yves Congar sums the
matter up well in saying, "Very solid connections are even revealed by
searching the Scriptures, not so much for passages supporting each
particular point immediately and critically, as for indications of the
overall sense of God's actions and will."[62] Beliefs and practices may
be supported by analogies, hints, and types, as well as by the overall
sense of Scripture. They do not necessarily need explicit statements
in Scripture to ground them. In fact, since much of Scripture comes
in narrative form, the most suitable way to go from the sacred text to
sacred doctrine is often through inferences drawn from the narrative
rather than through deductions based on propositions.[63] The goal is
to think biblically rather than simply cite Scripture.[64] In this light,
grounding a theology involves more than just piling up the greatest
number of explicit texts in support of one view over another, as if
having ten verses for one view automatically trumps a view that has
only three verses in its favor.[65] Furthermore, Kelsey reminds us that
doctrines need not "begin" with Scripture. They may begin with a
question or insight from outside the Bible, but at some point they will
invoke Scripture to authorize the proposal. This is not immediately
problematic since ideas can be true even if not found in the Bible.[66]

61. Turretin, *Institutes*, 1:37.

62. Yves Congar, *The Meaning of Tradition* (San Francisco: Ignatius, 2004), 39.

63. McGrath, *Genesis of Doctrine*, 61–63.

64. This point is made about the church fathers' use of Scripture in Richard A.
Muller, *The Study of Theology: From Biblical Interpretation to Contemporary Formulation* (Grand Rapids: Zondervan, 1991), 176.

65. See Lints, *Fabric of Theology*, 68–69.

66. Frame reminds students of this elusive truism, among other helpful hints, in
John M. Frame, *The Doctrine of the Knowledge of God* (Phillipsburg, NJ: P&R,
1987), 369–70.

Thus rather than thinking in terms of authoritative *beginnings* (although that is a valid concern), it would be better to consider whether a theology receives its authoritative *direction* from Scripture—that is, whether it is decisively shaped by or is at least consistent with the Christian narrative and its key themes, concerns, and emphases.

Perhaps a complicated distinction must then be made between what is binding and what is permissible. Doctrines are binding when they follow the clear sense of Scripture and can be shown to be rooted therein. Doctrines are permissible, perhaps, when they are not clearly taught in Scripture yet are still not inconsistent with it. The issue of permissible doctrines is what lies behind much of the debate between Catholics and Protestants and between various branches of Protestantism regarding how the Bible's authority can be expressed vis-à-vis things not addressed clearly in Scripture, such as certain church practices. All these distinctions are meant not to undermine the need to show one's work but to nuance what showing one's work might look like in practice.

7. *Measured judgment.* Keeping in mind the above discussion, the reader of theology is called on to make a judgment—a measured judgment, but a judgment nonetheless. It should be clear from our discussion that matters are rarely black and white. So the road to making measured judgments begins with recognizing that we are dealing in *degrees* of plausibility or strength. A theology's relation to Scripture is a major, if not *the* major, consideration for its relative plausibility.

As we assess this dimension of a proposal, we must keep in mind that we ourselves are judging from some standpoint. Thus *our* doctrine of Scripture and what matters in Scripture will largely affect our judgments. Nevertheless, we must put theology under the gaze of Scripture and ask about its attentiveness to the parts and whole of the Bible. Those theologies with clear connection to Scripture are stronger, even if one ultimately disagrees with them.

If the theology takes its direction in some meaningful ways from Scripture—for example, in its canonical awareness—it cannot be discounted as unchristian or implausible. It may not have as much exegetical, canonical, and metathematic backing as another proposal, but it cannot be rejected altogether as a non-option. However, some theological formulations will prove to be weakly rooted in God's revelation in Scripture, and we must be able to recognize this weakness. The ability to make such judgments requires that readers of theology grow in their own grasp of Scripture, so that their judgments can be made with humble confidence.

Conclusion: From Children's Song to Guiding Principle

The burden of this chapter was to affirm *sola Scriptura*, show variations in how it is applied in theology, and offer some principles for discerning how or if a theology accords with Scripture. The mainstream Christian tradition believes that Scripture must bear authoritatively on doctrine, but how it bears on doctrine takes numerous forms. One of the most common ways of relating the Bible to theological proposals is the proof-text. At its best, this is a nuanced appeal to Scripture (that is, to its manifold literal sense); at its worst, it is a way of justifying a preconceived theological agenda. The issues raised in the first three sections of the chapter were designed to foster caution and encourage nuance in theological students, who sometimes rush to make judgments on the basis of misinformation or an incomplete understanding of the attendant issues. The principles outlined at the end of the chapter represent a range of issues to consider when reading any theological proposal. The ultimate goal is that the principles become second nature instead of functioning like a checklist, even if they may have to perform that function for the time being. As the application of these principles bears the fruit of wisdom, may we be able to say yes, no, or maybe because we know what it means that "the Bible tells me so."

4

Haven't We Heard This Before?

Theology and Tradition

The recovery of the past is now treated as an arcane science.
—Marilynne Robinson, *The Death of Adam*

The undermining of the old orthodoxy has been mainly
the work of divines engaged in New Testament criticism.
The authority of experts in that discipline is the authority in deference to whom we are asked to give up a huge
mass of beliefs shared in common by the early Church,
the Fathers, the Middle Ages, the Reformers, and even
the nineteenth century.
—C. S. Lewis, *The Seeing Eye and Other
Selected Essays from Christian Reflections*

In the 1990s film *Groundhog Day*, local weatherman Phil Connors
is sent, for the fourth year in a row, to the small town of Punxsutawney, Pennsylvania, to report on its annual Groundhog Day celebra-
tions. Phil hates the town and resents having to spend another minute

covering a story that is clearly beneath him. After his news crew wraps
up shooting, they head out of town but are met with a snowstorm that
forces them to stay another night. When Phil wakes up the following
morning, he is quickly made aware that it is February 2, Groundhog
Day—again. As he walks through the day, he notices it unfolding in
the exact same way it did the previous day. He is living the very same
day and would do so day after day after day. No matter the events
or outcome of one day, he would return again to February 2 as if
nothing had happened. A miserable fate: trapped in Punxsutawney
. . . on Groundhog Day . . . for eternity.

Phil's situation is made more interesting by the fact that he is
the only person initially aware that he is reliving the day, a fact not
without its benefits. For example, each reboot does not wipe out his
memory, thus giving him the ability to accumulate detailed knowledge
of all the townspeople and acquire several skills like playing the piano
and speaking French. And when he sees how his cruelest and most
harmful acts have a negative effect lasting only twenty-four hours at
most, he insults people, schemes, and even commits suicide several
times, only to find himself back at Groundhog Day.

Phil's main interest, other than breaking the cycle in which he is
trapped, is winning the affections of his lovely coworker, Rita. She
becomes the first person he lets in on his little secret, exclaiming to
her, "I'm a god. I'm not *the* God . . . I don't think. . . . I have been
stabbed, shot, poisoned, frozen, hung, electrocuted, and burned. . . .
Every morning I wake up without a scratch on me, not a dent in the
fender. I am an immortal." Although skeptical at first, Rita comes
to believe him and convinces him to use his abilities—his recurring
days—for good rather than selfishly. He takes up her challenge and
goes on to use his godlike powers to help a choking man, save a boy
falling from a tree, attempt to prevent a homeless man from dying, and
perform countless other humanitarian acts toward the townspeople.
Thus begins Phil's transformation from a self-centered, self-seeking
misanthrope to a beloved man of the people.

Day by day, and through much failure, he also endears himself to
Rita, who is now drawn to this changed man. One evening, after a
Groundhog Day event, Phil and Rita return to his room. The film
picks up the next morning as they wake up together to find it is now

February 3. The cycle, the nightmare, is broken. And the couple rides off into the sunset to (presumably) live happily ever after.[1]

● ● ● ● ●

We have heard the saying that those who do not learn from the past are doomed to repeat it. For Phil, the old adage proves true: he quite literally must learn from his past if he is to ever break out of it. Initially, he sees returning to the past as pure misery. His life is changed, however, when he realizes that returning to the past with the right perspective can make for a brighter future. What we learn from Phil is that if the past is seen as a set of failures from which we may or may not draw lessons, "doom" is a fitting way to describe being consigned to it. Yet like him, we must realize that the past is not something to which we are doomed; it is not punishment or a burden. Rather, the past can be the very doorway to wisdom for the future. As Marilynne Robinson writes, "I do not wish to suggest . . . that the past was better than the present, simply that whatever in the past happens to have been of significance or value ought to be held in memory, insofar as that is possible, so that it can give us guidance."[2] The past can be our guide.

This moral is no less true in theology. Theologians have always recognized that their work is done in conversation with the past. This is the "secondary conversation" mentioned earlier by Barth.[3] Theology, when done well, is always a retrieval project: it seeks to mine the Christian past for theological riches that will benefit the present and the future of the church. Retrieval does not equate with agreement but at the very least connotes dialogue. To put the matter another way, responsible theology engages with what we would call "the tradition"—the "faith transmitted by the community of interpreters that has preceded us."[4] In the previous chapter, we explored

1. See "Synopsis for *Groundhog Day*" at http://www.imdb.com/title/tt0107048 /synopsis.
2. Marilynne Robinson, *The Death of Adam: Essays on Modern Thought*, reprint ed. (New York: Picador, 2005), 5.
3. Karl Barth, *Evangelical Theology: An Introduction*, trans. Grover Foley (Grand Rapids: Eerdmans, 1979), 174. See chap. 1 of the present work.
4. Richard Lints, *The Fabric of Theology: A Prolegomenon to Evangelical Theology* (Eugene, OR: Wipf and Stock, 1999), 84.

various ways theologians interact with Scripture as they do theology. The chief aim of this chapter is to illuminate how theologians and theologies relate to tradition in its various forms, which will provide categories for assessing the cogency of theological proposals. The first section of the chapter examines various problems related to the place of tradition in theological formulation and offers some reflections on why it must be a conversation partner in theology. I then outline four distinct categories that tend to be treated under the rubric of tradition—creeds, confessions, doctors, and other theologians—and how they each uniquely factor into theological proposals. Finally, I offer a taxonomy of what I call theological "genres"—a categorizing of theologies based on how they self-consciously relate to tradition. The chapter concludes by bringing together the preceding reflections into several broad principles for evaluating theologies in relation to tradition.

Why Tradition?

Thus far I have kept our definition of tradition fairly general. However, it would be helpful to offer a fuller definition of what theologians mean when they speak of "tradition." McGrath describes it as the handing down of the kerygma (apostolic preaching) within the community of faith.[5] A. N. Williams defines tradition as "the church's sacred teaching, which undergoes at least linguistic reformulation over time, and which interprets the Bible in light of the church's worship, experience of the living God, and practice of the Christian life." It is the "communal interpretation of the Bible which is above all, though not exclusively, doctrinal in content."[6] Recognizing that not defining terms—in this case "tradition"—engenders some unnecessary conflicts about its place in theology and church practice, post-Reformation Lutheran theologian Martin Chemnitz proposes eight ways one could understand the term: (1) what Christ spoke to his apostles; (2) the faithful

5. Alister E. McGrath, *The Genesis of Doctrine: A Study in the Foundation of Doctrinal Criticism* (Grand Rapids: Eerdmans, 1997), 173.
6. A. N. Williams, "Tradition," in *The Oxford Handbook of Systematic Theology*, ed. John Webster, Kathryn Tanner, and Iain Torrance (New York: Oxford University Press, 2009), 363.

passing on of the Scriptures; (3) the apostolic traditions preserved in the churches; (4) the proper exposition and interpretation of Scripture; (5) dogmas that are implied in Scripture or brought together by sound, biblical reasoning; (6) the catholic consensus of the church fathers; (7) ancient rites/practices that can be traced back to the apostles; and (8) authoritative doctrines and practices that *cannot* be traced back to Scripture.[7] Definitions abound. Yet for all the relative diversity, there is at least one common thread: tradition's close relation to the Bible. The relation of these two authorities has a long and complicated history, but it is one we must examine if we are to grasp tradition's normative role in the formulation of theology.

Scripture and Tradition

The main concern regarding the authority of tradition, historically speaking, is that it is sometimes seen as posing a threat to the supreme authority of Scripture. This represents the first challenge to the place of tradition in theology. Throughout the history of the church, the relationship between the two authorities—Scripture and tradition—has been rich but by no means straightforward. Anthony Lane outlines five ways the relationship has been conceived historically.[8] Knowing these perspectives can help orient the reader to the underlying assumptions of the theology in question.

1. *The coincidence view.* This was the predominant view in the early church, as seen in the writings of Irenaeus and Tertullian. According to this position, the apostolic tradition—that

---

7. Chemnitz accepts all but the last option, in contrast to his reading of the Council of Trent. Martin Chemnitz, *Chemnitz's Works, Volume 1: Examination of the Council of Trent*, trans. Fred Kramer (St. Louis: Concordia, 2008), 217–307.

8. Much of this discussion is drawn from Anthony N. S. Lane, "Scripture, Tradition and Church: An Historical Survey," *Vox Evangelica* 9 (1975): 37–55; and Lane, "Tradition," in *Dictionary for Theological Interpretation of the Bible*, ed. Kevin J. Vanhoozer et al. (Grand Rapids: Baker Academic, 2005), 809–12. Others like Heiko Oberman or Keith Mathison give a two- or threefold taxonomy. See Heiko Oberman, *Forerunners of the Reformation: The Shape of Late Medieval Thought, Illustrated by Key Documents*, trans. Paul L. Nyhus (New York: Holt, Rinehart & Winston, 1966), 51–65; and Keith A. Mathison, *The Shape of Sola Scriptura* (Moscow, ID: Canon, 2001).

which was taught orally by the apostles and preserved in the churches—does not add to the Scriptures but coincides with them, revealing how they are to be interpreted. In this view, Scripture does not stand as judge over the tradition, nor can the two be opposed to each other. Instead, they are always mutually confirming, since their content is identical.

2. *The supplementary view.* This position holds that certain things, such as liturgy and ritual practices, were passed on to the churches by the apostles but are not taught explicitly in Scripture. Thus tradition adds to Scripture, not speaking contrary to it per se but rather supplementing its teachings where it appears silent. This view had some prominent representatives, such as Augustine and Basil, can be traced as far back as the *Didache* and *The Apostolic Tradition*, and is a common understanding of post-Reformation Roman Catholicism.

3. *The ancillary view.* This is the view held by the magisterial Reformers (broadly speaking). According to this view, tradition's authority is binding only if consistent with the clear teachings of Scripture. It differs from the coincidence view in three main ways: (a) it does not assume that the teaching of church, tradition, and Scripture will be identical; (b) it assumes that tradition is reformable; and (c) it accords authority to the tradition not because it claims apostolic origin but because it can be found in Scripture.

4. *The solitary view.* This position is often wrongly equated with the slogan *sola Scriptura*. This radicalized version of the Reformation principle, held by some Anabaptists and Brethren believers, is hostile or indifferent to tradition and seeks to give Scripture sole authority in the church, not heeding the church's history of biblical interpretation.

5. *The unfolding view.* This view is a result of the growing recognition in Catholic circles that some doctrines have the clear support of neither Scripture nor early Christian tradition. The idea thus arose that certain doctrines develop or unfold over time. Only the seed of a doctrine need be found in Scripture or early tradition—a notion that some call "implicit tradition."

Over time, what only existed in seed form, as implicit tradition, blooms full flower into the explicit teaching of the church. In other words, the fullest understanding of theological truth unfolds gradually throughout history, so that the present understanding of the truth is richer than what was held before. The immaculate conception of Mary or Mary's bodily assumption are prime examples of such developed doctrines.

What this brief sketch highlights is that faithful Christian theologians differ in their conceptions of the relationship between Scripture and tradition in theological formulation. How theologians understand this relationship will significantly shape how and what they draw from either source and consequently how we approach assessing their theological proposals. For example, if theologians hold the solitary view, we should not expect to find them highly conversant with traditional sources. Although we are justified to deem that neglect unfortunate and shortsighted, we must initially be able to address the theology on its own terms. Similarly, if theologians operate according to the unfolding view, readers should expect that certain doctrines will have a thinner or, better, a less apparent scriptural foundation. Thus, recognizing our view of this relationship as well as that of the theologian we are engaging can go a long way toward reading critically and charitably.

The Problem(s) of Tradition

The authority of tradition in theology has been challenged historically by two camps: (1) those who view it as stifling reason and (2) those who see it as usurping Scripture's rightful place.[9] The first camp describes tradition as a poor substitute for reason and views any appeals to it as obscurantist and repressive. This view is representative of the Enlightenment ideal that only what cannot be doubted should be accepted, in contrast to blind belief in the authority of tradition.[10]

9. To these we could add a third camp that argues that tradition stifles one's own experience. I address the relationship of experience to Scripture in chap. 6. The comments there can be applied to tradition's relationship to experience.

10. Richard Bauckham, "Tradition in Relation to Scripture and Reason," in *Scripture, Tradition and Reason: A Study in the Criteria of Christian Doctrine*, ed. Richard Bauckham and Benjamin Drewery (Edinburgh: T&T Clark, 1988), 132.

For those with this temperament, the past is seen not as a resource but rather as an "intellectual charnel house for ideas now obsolete."[11] This view correctly asserts the need for each person to own their beliefs rather than have them forcibly imposed. Moreover, traditions theological or otherwise are (at least in principle) revisable and should be evaluated critically.[12] However, the critiques are overblown, for there are several problems with this prejudice against tradition. First, this view is naive. It fails to see that all reasoning happens within the context of a particular tradition of thought. Human minds are shaped by social living and shared conceptions of rationality; that is, they do not proceed as if starting from scratch. This is true even in the sciences, where knowledge and methods are handed down. These "traditions" can then be critiqued, appropriated, or advanced, but rarely avoided. Scientific inquiry is conditioned by the tradition that preceded it. In fact, even what we would call rational is often only so for those inhabiting a particular tradition.[13] Second, this view is ambiguous. When we oppose tradition to reason, we perpetuate certain ambiguities regarding the nature of each. For instance, tradition surely includes reason in that it includes the thought of some of the greatest thinkers in history. Moreover, whatever we mean by reason is usually some tradition of reasoning, such as Platonist, Aristotelian, idealist, realist, Kantian, and so forth. In each case, reason reveals itself to be socially and historically conditioned or, put differently, traditioned.[14] While more could be said, philosopher Alasdair MacIntyre sums up the issue well when he writes, "What I am, therefore, is in key part what I inherit, a specific past that is present to some degree in my present. I find myself part of a history and that is generally to say, whether I like it or not, whether I recognize it or not, one of the bearers of a tradition."[15] Reason cannot, and for its own sake should not, attempt to escape the so-called shackles of tradition. Sanctified Christian reason operates within the sphere of a tradition handed down to us, and it is better for it.

11. McGrath, *Genesis of Doctrine*, 166.
12. McGrath, *Genesis of Doctrine*, 180, 185.
13. McGrath, *Genesis of Doctrine*, 180–82.
14. Bauckham, "Tradition," 139–40.
15. Alasdair MacIntyre, *After Virtue: A Study in Moral Theory*, 2nd ed. (Notre Dame: University of Notre Dame Press, 1984), 221.

The authority of tradition is challenged from a second direction, namely, from those adopting the solitary view outlined earlier. While many in this camp would not see themselves as sympathetic to the Enlightenment project, they similarly argue that appeals to tradition betray an irrational circumvention of first principles—in this case, the primacy of Scripture. The desire among those who hold this view is to keep theology and church practice tethered to the Bible as closely as possible, without the sometimes-damaging influence of tradition. Adherents of this view are driven to keep the church pure by repeatedly calling it back to Scripture. One of their chief fears is what might be called *traditionalism*, a perspective that sees tradition (1) as unchangeable or incorrigible—even by Scripture—once it has been established and (2) as authoritative as Scripture.[16] However, Lints calls this bent "antitraditional traditionalism" because it seeks to keep the church moored to its roots (i.e., it is traditional) and to do so by ignoring the centuries between the first and the present one (i.e., it is antitraditional). The question framing this view is, "Why can we not simply do theology from the Bible alone?" In responding to this valid question, I will offer a positive account of the place of tradition in theology, not merely as a historical fact but as a central principle.

The Promise of Tradition

Is it possible or desirable to do theology solely from Scripture without the strong hand of tradition guiding us along? Most theologians of the past would respond with a resounding no to the suggestion. Tradition has been and should be a serious consideration in theological formulation for several reasons. First, it is unavoidable. As mentioned in the previous chapter, Bible-only churches will inevitably establish their own traditions of reading and practicing the Bible, often dictated by one pastor or influential leader, who in turn functions authoritatively in church life. As A. A. Hodge puts it, "The real question is not, as often pretended, between the Word of God and the creed of man, but between the tried and proved faith of the collective body of God's people, and the private judgment and

16. John M. Frame, *The Doctrine of the Word of God* (Phillipsburg, NJ: P&R, 2010), 282.

the unassisted wisdom of the repudiator of creeds."[17] Tradition is inevitable. The question is whether we will be guided by a good one or a poor one. Theologians have often found that listening to the tradition is a more fruitful avenue into knowing the Scriptures than merely consulting modern Bible commentators or (worse) themselves. Past readers of the Bible open our eyes to things we may miss because of the cultural logs blinding our view. In addition, even if we were able to read the Bible unencumbered by tradition, we would quickly find that the Bible itself is already mediated to us through traditions such as the following:

- The tradition of Bible translation
- The tradition of grammar and syntax (of Greek, Hebrew, or Aramaic)
- The accumulated wisdom found in lexicons
- The tradition(s) of textual criticism that gives us our Greek New Testament[18]

The point is that if we tried to go straight to the Bible, even in the original languages, tradition would be unavoidable.

The second reason for heeding tradition in theology is ecclesiological: we are in fact connected to those who came before us. Past theologians are members of the body of Christ and are still alive. Our work should not be done with intentional ignorance of those theologians who are acknowledged as significant in shaping the church's knowledge of the gospel. The voices of past saints should be listened to as if they were the voices of contemporary brothers and sisters in Christ. We share the same ecclesial context and must converse with them respectfully.[19] Thus though dead, they still speak and may

17. A. A. Hodge, *The Confession of Faith: A Handbook of Christian Doctrine Expounding the Westminster Confession* (London: Banner of Truth, 1961), 2.

18. Stephen R. Holmes, *Listening to the Past: The Place of Tradition in Theology* (Carlisle, UK: Paternoster; Grand Rapids: Baker Academic, 2002), 6–7. One might also include the social traditions of the culture in which we live. For example, see E. Randolph Richards and Brandon J. O'Brien, *Misreading Scripture with Western Eyes: Removing Cultural Blinders to Better Understand the Bible* (Downers Grove, IL: InterVarsity, 2012).

19. Holmes, *Listening to the Past*, 30–31.

continue to help bring the church to full maturity and unity in Christ. "To refuse to learn from the tradition in doing theology," writes Stephen Holmes, "is to succumb to the pride that says 'because you are not a hand, I don't need you,' and to spurn the most excellent way of love, without which all insight and all knowledge is only precisely nothing."[20]

The third and most important reason for giving place to tradition in theological formulation is that our creatureliness demands it. The fact that we stand at this moment in time rather than another is a limitation that expresses itself in our inability to access the apostolic witness to Christ in a direct and unmediated fashion. We access it through the tradition of the church. If this limitation is a result of the fall, it should be resisted. However, if it is part and parcel of being a creature, it is good and should be embraced. If we accept, with theologians like Irenaeus, that God created the world with time and movement toward eschatological perfection, then history and our situatedness in it are intended by God. We are creatures, in time, embedded in history. Moreover, the doctrine of the incarnation tells us that limited creaturely existence is a good embraced by God himself. Jesus was subject to a particular moment in history and to growth and development (in knowledge, stature, and favor with God and others; Luke 2:52). Time, change, development, limits—these are part of the good created order. In light of this, where we are in history, separated from the apostles by a long tradition, is actually proper to our being as humans and is very good. Thus the mediated nature of our knowledge of the New Testament's witness, namely, the *handing on* of the gospel from generation to generation, is something to be celebrated rather than repudiated. Knowledge of the past is gained not by an ahistorical flight but by taking seriously the history through which the past is made known to us.

According to its critics, tradition is either irrelevant or untrue, and appeals to it are either irrational or unfaithful.[21] However, as

---

20. Holmes, *Listening to the Past*, 34.

21. Referring to Anglican divine Richard Hooker's view of tradition, McGrath writes, "If tradition merely restates what can be established through scripture and reason, it is redundant; if it states anything which is 'neither in scripture, nor can otherwise sufficiently by any reason be proved to be of God,' it has forfeited its claim

we have seen, tradition is an unavoidable and indispensable dialogue partner and resource in doing theology responsibly. Thus knowing the Christian tradition and recognizing theology's constant interactions with it are necessary skills for anyone desiring to critically engage doctrine.

Which Tradition? Four Categories

Thus far we have described tradition and offered some rationale for its important place in theological reflection. Yet some ambiguity remains in our use of the term "tradition." When theologians speak about tradition, they may have several different things in view. "Tradition" may refer to ecumenical creeds, confessions of faith, doctors of the church, or any theologian in the church's history. Each of these is an important facet of the church's tradition, yet they differ in their relative authority.[22] At one end of the spectrum, some traditions are almost universally recognized as normative. On the other end are traditions that are viewed as merely helpful. In between are traditions that function normatively among some groups but not among others. In this section, we will explore these four categories of tradition and examine how they differ in their authority and use in the practice of theology.

Creeds

Creeds are public statements that define what is necessary for salvation or for the well-being of the church, usually in the face of some controversy or dispute.[23] By "creeds" I refer chiefly to those documents produced by ecumenical councils in the early centuries of the church,

---

to truth. Tradition is therefore at best unnecessary, and at worst untrue." G. R. Evans, Alister E. McGrath, and Alan D. Galloway, *The Science of Theology* (Basingstoke, UK: Marshall Pickering, 1986), 183.

22. As theologian Don Thorsen observes, tradition is "an uneven pool of reliable religious authority." Here the author is referring to John Wesley's view of tradition. See Don Thorsen, *The Wesleyan Quadrilateral: Scripture, Tradition, Reason and Experience as a Model of Evangelical Theology* (Lexington: Emeth, 2005), 101.

23. Philip Schaff and David S. Schaff, *The Creeds of Christendom*, 3 vols., 6th ed. (Grand Rapids: Baker, 1931), 1:3–4.

particularly Nicaea I (325), Constantinople I (381), Ephesus (431), and Chalcedon (451). To these, most would add the Apostles' Creed. These are accepted as normative by most Eastern Orthodox, Roman Catholic, and Protestant bodies.[24]

Reflecting on the first council, T. F. Torrance captures the uniqueness of the statements these councils produced. "The council of Nicaea of 325 AD has a unique place in the history of the Christian Church as . . . 'the Great Ecumenical Synod' to which all subsequent Ecumenical Councils looked back as their normative basis. The Nicene Creed secured the apostolic and catholic faith against disrupting distortions of the Gospel in a decisive form that eventually commanded and unified the mind of the whole Church."[25] He goes on to say that the council was believed to be so directed by the Spirit that Athanasius (and others) could refer to the creed as "the Word of the Lord" that "abides forever."[26] The affirmations of the church in the first five centuries have received universal assent and are thus accorded a status above any other tradition. In addressing the question of how to discern true catholic teaching from false, Vincent of Lérins proposes the following criteria: "All possible care must be taken, that we hold that faith which has been believed everywhere, always, by all."[27] Sure teaching is that which can claim universality, antiquity, and consent: (1) it is universally recognized (in terms of geography); (2) it has an ancient pedigree (from the first few centuries); and (3) it has secured the agreement of most of the ancient doctors and fathers of the church.[28]

It is easy to see, if we adopt anything like Vincent's "canon," that the ecumenical creeds are the clearest standard of true, orthodox Christian teaching. They achieved (and continue to receive) the

24. Eastern Orthodox communions also receive the next three councils (Constantinople II and III and Nicaea II) as authoritative. Roman Catholics receive these three as well as all councils up to Vatican II. Protestants would accord some authority only to Constantinople III. See Williams, "Tradition," 374.

25. Thomas F. Torrance, *Trinitarian Faith: The Evangelical Theology of the Ancient Catholic Faith*, new ed. (Edinburgh: T&T Clark, 1995), 13.

26. Torrance, *Trinitarian Faith*, 15.

27. Vincent of Lérins, "Commonitorium," chap. 2, trans. C. A. Heurtley, http://www.newadvent.org/fathers/3506.htm.

28. Vincent of Lérins, "Commonitorium," chap. 2.

consent of the whole church during the pivotal formative stages of Christianity. Moreover, these statements were forged in a time, place, culture, and language close in proximity to the founding of the church. If the authority of tradition is unevenly distributed, most weight resides in the creeds of the church.[29] Scripture is the ultimate authority; the creeds are subordinate authorities.

While creeds have the authority of a herald, not a magistrate, they have real and binding authority.[30] There is unlikely to be a biblical, historical, logical, or experiential argument strong enough to cause us to reject any clause in the creeds, particularly since they have been recited, lived out, and passed on by billions through many centuries and in almost every possible context, and no such arguments have proved compelling.[31] Thus the Christian consensus—or "mere Christianity," to borrow a phrase from C. S. Lewis—embodied in the ecumenical creeds of the first five centuries provides the minimal guidelines by which we judge the relative Christian-ness of any theological proposal.

Confessions

Although creeds and confessions both declare the faith, confessions are more parochial in character. For example, the Belgic Confession is a Reformed statement, while the Formula of Concord is Lutheran. These statements are normative within their particular communions because they are believed to encapsulate a corporate understanding of the whole counsel of God in Scripture. They function similarly to ecumenical creeds but are less authoritative because they do not share the universal consent and antiquity characteristic of the creeds.

29. Anglican bishop Lancelot Andrewes captures an ecumenical sentiment: "One canon reduced to writing by God himself, two testaments, three creeds, four general councils, five centuries, and the series of fathers in that period—the three centuries, that is, before Constantine, and two after, determine the boundary of our faith." Quoted in Robert L. Ottley, *Lancelot Andrewes* (London: Methuen, 1894), 163. Though, again, certain traditions would add other creedal statements to this shared affirmation.

30. John Webster, *Confessing God: Essays in Christian Dogmatics II*, 2nd ed. (London: T&T Clark, 2016), 81–82.

31. Holmes, *Listening to the Past*, 157–60.

Doctors

Throughout the history of the church, certain individual theologians have been recognized as "heroes," those especially helpful in guiding the church in its understanding of the gospel. Just as biographies of saints provide models of how to live as Christians, so "doctors" provide examples of how to think in a Christian manner. And just as saints' biographies do not add to the gospel but rather bring out certain dimensions of it more fully, so the work of these recognized teachers illumines aspects of the faith without adding to it.[32] The category of "doctor" has a historical pedigree, referring to officially recognized saintly teachers in the Catholic Church and to those responsible for the instruction of the church beyond a particular locality among the Reformed.[33] The term here simply refers to the universally recognized major players, the real influencers of Christian thought and practice throughout the ages.

Not surprisingly, in light of our discussion above, the fathers of the early centuries of the church receive a proportionately greater amount of deference than other doctors. Someone is a doctor or a work is a "classic" when (1) many people in a particular context judge a work or a writer as uniquely successful and convincing in their presentation of the gospel and its logic; (2) other theologians deem the writer as particularly insightful and seminal; (3) the agreement regarding a particular writer spans different times and contexts; or (4) the agreement spans theological traditions to include those who disagree on other points of doctrine.[34]

What kind of authority do these teachers have with respect to contemporary theological reflection? While sharing with creeds and confessions a measure of universal recognition, each particular point of their teaching is subject to greater scrutiny, since it is not the product of communal discernment and consensus. Their authority is real, but it is the authority of an eminently wise yet fallible minister. Calvin insists that they are our servants, not lords, that

32. Holmes, *Listening to the Past*, 28–29.
33. See Kevin J. Vanhoozer, *Pictures at a Theological Exhibition: Scenes of the Church's Worship, Witness and Wisdom* (Downers Grove, IL: IVP Academic, 2016), 59–62.
34. Holmes, *Listening to the Past*, 157–58.

what they wrote is for our good, and that we are free to receive or reject what they propound. They "were ignorant of many things, often disagreed among themselves, and sometimes even contradicted themselves."[35] No argument is settled by mere appeal to a doctor. Yet a wise use of our freedom with respect to them is to listen to these acclaimed experts as guides into the mysteries of the faith.

Other Teachers

Theology is often done in conversation with figures from the past who do not quite qualify as doctors or fathers but are nonetheless significant theological resources. They differ from doctors in the degree of authority they exert, not the kind, and they contribute to the richness of the Christian tradition. But what kind of influence and authority do they exert on theology? It seems these writers perform the basic function of being thoughtful dialogue partners and fellow travelers from a different era. While holding much in common with us, they are not subject to the assumptions and blind spots of our age. C. S. Lewis's counsel on reading old books in general applies to our engagement with past theologians in particular (and I quote at length):

> None of us can fully escape this blindness, but we shall certainly increase it, and weaken our guard against it, if we read only modern books. Where they are true they will give us truths which we half knew already. Where they are false they will aggravate the error with which we are already dangerously ill. The only palliative is . . . [reading] old books. Not, of course, that there is any magic about the past. People were no cleverer then than they are now; they made as many mistakes as we. But not the same mistakes. They will not flatter us in the errors we are already committing; and their own errors, being now open and palpable, will not endanger us.[36]

35. John Calvin, *Calvin: Institutes of the Christian Religion*, ed. John T. McNeill, trans. Ford Lewis Battles (Louisville: Westminster John Knox, 1960), 18–19.
36. From the essay "On the Reading of Old Books," in C. S. Lewis, *First and Second Things: Essays in Theology and Ethics*, ed. Walter Hooper (Glasgow: Collins, 1985), 28.

Theology in conversation is not de facto correct, but it is stronger than theology as a monologue. Past theologians and writers are a gift to present theological reflection. They help us to faithfully live out the gospel in our day by clearing out the cultural assumptions that get in the way of our vocation.

Theological Genres

If you have read theology even for a little while, you will notice that theologians interact with tradition in different ways—some sympathetically, some critically; others follow it closely, while others do so loosely. We can label these various modes of interaction "genres." In chapter 2, we explored the need to attend to authors' contexts. We discovered that knowing context helps to limit the range of interpretive possibilities, but it also opens up new vistas of understanding otherwise unavailable to the theological student.

This is no less true in the case of genres. C. S. Lewis speaks of what he calls "serious" reading, highlighting that readers should "read 'in the same spirit that the author writ.' What is meant lightly he will take lightly; what is meant gravely, gravely."[37] Lewis points out that readers need to be attentive to the kind of text they are reading. Those he calls "literary Puritans" read every text *too* seriously, oblivious to genre. One text on biblical interpretation calls this necessary attentiveness *literary competence*, which is defined as "the ability to discern cues within the text that indicate what kind of literature we are working with and, hence, what to expect or not to expect from it."[38] Gordon Fee and Douglas Stuart similarly write that genre differences "are vital and should affect both the way one reads them and how one is to understand their message for today."[39]

The literary Puritan is someone who reads all writings as if they were the same kind of thing. Thus their expectations of what they

---

37. C. S. Lewis, *An Experiment in Criticism* (repr., Cambridge: Cambridge University Press, 2012), 11.

38. William W. Klein et al., *Introduction to Biblical Interpretation* (Dallas: Word, 1993), 260.

39. Gordon D. Fee and Douglas Stuart, *How to Read the Bible for All Its Worth*, 4th ed. (Grand Rapids: Zondervan, 2014), 17.

should receive from or see in a text are sometimes misguided. This principle applies to reading theology as well. Theologians approach the task of theologizing in a variety of ways. Each goes about it with particular aims in mind and adopts a style appropriate for those aims. We must be aware of the kind of thing we are working with: Is it experimental; is it conventional; is it constructive and suggestive? If we understand better what we are dealing with, we might be able to relax and avoid feeling some of the threats described in earlier chapters.

Toward that end, I propose five theological genres, or ways theologians self-consciously interact with the tradition. None represents a hard-and-fast category, for few whole theologies fit cleanly in any one genre. Moreover, no taxonomy of approaches is ever exhaustive. Yet by providing some taxonomy, I hope to increase literary competence and help the reader form appropriate expectations and criteria for assessing different theologies.[40]

Figure 4.1
Theological Genres

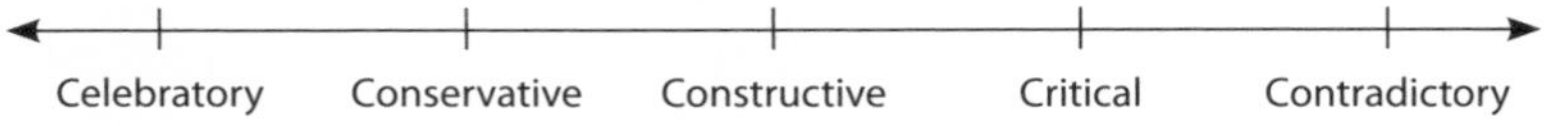

| Celebratory | Conservative | Constructive | Critical | Contradictory |

1. *Celebratory* theology. This is an attempt to put on display the beauty and riches of the faith for the purpose of evoking a "fullness of vision," a sense of awe and wonder. In this approach, the goal is not so much to argue as to exult in the rich imagery and the realities to which they point. Celebratory theology usually comes in the form of hymns and preaching, but it is also found in the work of quite rigorous theologians (much of the work of Hans Urs von Balthasar exemplifies this approach).[41]

40. For a threefold typology of how theologies relate to Scripture and tradition, see Gregory C. Higgins, *Christianity 101: A Textbook of Catholic Theology* (New York: Paulist Press, 2007), 11–24. Some readers might be familiar with Hans Frei's typology in *Types of Christian Theology*, ed. George Hunsinger and William Placher (New Haven: Yale University Press, 1992), 28–55, 116–32. Frei emphasizes chiefly academic theologies, their relation to philosophy, and the language of description they employ. I try to present a taxonomy that includes churchly forms of theology as well.

41. Taken from Rowan Williams, *On Christian Theology*, Challenges in Contemporary Theology (Malden, MA: Blackwell, 2000), xiii–xiv.

2. *Conservative* theology. I use this term not as the binary opposite of liberal nor as a term connoting any value. This type of
theology is concerned primarily with articulating and defending
the tradition as it has been handed down. The most basic form of
this genre is the creedal or confessional statement. Conservative
theologies are explanatory; they aim to make clear what is to
be believed. In this approach there is little concern for novelty;
perhaps there is even a suspicion of it. The language used in this
and the celebratory forms of theology tends to be more biblical-
theological or traditional, while its primary audience tends to
be churchly rather than academic. Many evangelical, Catholic,
and Orthodox theologies may be grouped in this category.

3. *Constructive* theology. A constructive approach views tradition
not merely as something to defend but also as something to wield;
it provides the substantive resources for addressing important
issues inside and outside the church. In this mode, theology
tends toward "obedient creativity": obedient to the teaching of
Scripture and its creedal appropriations but creative in extending
its implications. We see historical examples of this approach, for
instance, in the marshaling of classical Christology to address
medieval ecclesial questions regarding images and Reformation
debates concerning the Lord's Supper. In the latter case, Lutheran
and Reformed theologies extended the insights of fundamentally
Chalcedonian Christologies into their contemporary ecclesial
controversy. Similar potential exists for matters that have bearing
outside the church. This approach is taken by modern theologians like Colin Gunton, Jürgen Moltmann, and T. F. Torrance.[42]

4. *Critical* theology. This genre arises from the need to check the
church's speech about God—whether it has spoken out of step

42. Williams, *On Christian Theology*, xiv. Under the umbrella of constructive
theology is what Williams calls "communicative" theology: a theology that freely
uses the idioms and thought forms of its nonecclesial environment. He writes, "The
assumption is that this or that intellectual idiom not only offers a way into fruitful
conversation with the current environment but also that the unfamiliar idiom may
uncover aspects of the deposit of belief hitherto unexamined." The bent here can be
slightly apologetic, and the language and concepts are "borrowed" from the other
fields or disciplines. The early church apologists, Origen, and even contemporary
writers utilizing speech-act theory would fit into this category.

with the tradition or the tradition has spoken out of step with the truth. Apophatic (or negative) theology is a basic form of critical theology as it "sometimes [does] no more than [sound] a warning note against the idea that we could secure a firm grip upon definitions of the divine."[43] Critical theologies are concerned with raising questions about concepts, method, content, and whatever else in the tradition might be obscuring the church's confession and the realities to which theology points. As Calvin puts it, there is a difference between a disciple and an ape.[44] Tradition can be questioned, developed, critiqued. Moreover, this genre tends toward an academic audience (although not always), often using language and concepts borrowed from other disciplines. Critical theologies are deployed by those with a measure of freedom to ask unsettling questions from the outside, since they are not moored to the dictates of a particular tradition. Modern examples of this approach include Rudolf Bultmann and Elisabeth Schüssler Fiorenza.[45]

5. *Contradictory* theology. Critical theologies can sometimes terminate in a fifth genre, what might be called a contradictory mode, namely, the rejection of particular central Christian concepts, a particular Christian teaching, or Christian truth claims altogether. Gordon Kaufman and Don Cupitt are examples of this academic approach.[46] Since these theologies often lie outside the boundaries of self-conscious Christian reflection, they will not be our focus.

It should be mentioned again that entire theologies do not fit squarely in one category or another. Barth's *Church Dogmatics* is a fine example, for while his language draws primarily from the dogmatic tradition, its tone is sometimes exultant, sometimes constructive, and sometimes critical. One could find constructive moments in what is

---

43. Williams, *On Christian Theology*, xv.
44. Calvin's letter to Martin Seidemann, March 14, 1555, cited in B. A. Gerrish, *Thinking with the Church: Essays in Historical Theology* (Grand Rapids: Eerdmans, 2010), 122.
45. See Higgins, *Christianity 101*, 18–23.
46. See Williams, *On Christian Theology*, xv.

largely a conservative work or critical moments in a constructive work. Furthermore, one genre is not inherently better than the others, nor is any genre inherently inferior (with the possible exception of the contradictory genre). Theologians are responsible to their primary audiences, and their form of discourse will adapt accordingly.[47]

The church needs conservative and critical theologies (as well as the others) if it is to remain faithful to its calling. The point of this taxonomy is not to pigeonhole or make value judgments but to alert the reader to the variety of legitimate activities being done under the banner of "theology" and how theologies are shaped by their interaction with tradition. In the final section, I will expand on the implications of knowing genre and how that shapes our evaluation of theologies vis-à-vis tradition.

Theology and Tradition: Principles and Reflections

In this chapter, we have reflected on a variety of issues related to theology's interaction with the Christian tradition. In the process, I have hinted at how these reflections might shape our reading of theology. As a conclusion to the chapter, I would like to expand somewhat on those intimations and draw out some guiding principles from each of the sections above.

1. *Discern the assumed view of tradition.* Every theology assumes a particular understanding of tradition and how it relates to Scripture. Intelligent reading requires that we discern which view is operative. If a theology assumes a solitary view of tradition (i.e., that tradition has no place in theological formulation), then it is more difficult to detect the strands of tradition from which it draws (even though it will likely do so unwittingly). Along these lines, we must be aware of our own assumed understanding of tradition. If one holds a solitary view but is trying to interact with a theology that assumes the

---

47. Williams writes, "It is legitimate in the celebratory mode to imagine a believing public and to employ methods of internal elaboration of themes, refinement of imaginative patterns, and so on, without too much attention to 'critical' issues of conceptual clarity. . . . The critical theologian should not be deflected by considerations of conventional piety from challenging and testing the language of celebration." Williams, *On Christian Theology*, xv–xvi.

coincidence or developmental view, the reader must allow that this
theology will not be operating with the same constraint to appeal
to direct teachings of Scripture. This difference in fundamental assumptions can make evaluation frustrating but not impossible. The
frustration comes from the ease with which we will be able to talk
past one another. On the other hand, we will have a deeper understanding of *why* the two parties disagree on this or that teaching.
In the end, we must assess theologies on their own terms as well as
on the basis of criteria that might be foreign to them, that is, on the
basis of our preferred understanding of tradition.

2. *Ascribe the authority appropriate to the tradition.* The canon
of Vincent of Lérins, that a doctrine is to be believed if it "has been
believed everywhere, always, by all," moves us forward but only gets
us so far. He establishes a solid principle that all Christian teaching
must agree with the consensus of the early church as stated in the
creeds. What happens, however, when the matter under discussion is
not mentioned in the creeds but does not contradict the creeds? To
this Vincent responds that the reader

> must collate and consult and interrogate the opinions of the ancients,
> of those, namely, who, though living in various times and places yet
> continuing in the communion and faith of the one Catholic church,
> stand forth acknowledged and approved authorities: and whatsoever
> he shall ascertain to have been held, written, taught, not by one or two
> of these only, but by all, equally, with one consent, openly, frequently,
> persistently, that he must understand that he himself also is to believe
> without any doubt or hesitation.[48]

If the creeds do not speak to it, then consult the opinions of a *group*
of acknowledged authorities. If the creeds do not mention something,
discover what the doctors (note: plural) have to say. And whatever they
agree on, we must see as the standard. I would include communal
documents like confessions because they represent the wisdom of a
community of faith rather than the opinions of a single author. If
a theology can be shown to be consistent with or rooted in creeds,
confessions, or doctors, then it is on the right track. But what about

48. Vincent of Lérins, "Commonitorium," chap. 3.

the tradition of lesser lights, or other teachers? If a theology is not entirely novel, in that it has been taught by one orthodox theologian or another in the past, and if it has never been denounced by the church, then it is worthy of our attention as a possible interpretation of the faith. Even if it is unlikely that this theology will prove superior to more well-worn and accepted teachings, it should be accorded the respect of a dialogue partner. To put the matter simply, we should ask the following questions:

- Does the theology contradict the ecumenical creeds?
- If not addressed by the creeds, is it consistent with them?
- Are there other communal documents (i.e., confessions) that follow this view?
- Are there any prominent doctors who hold this view? Only one, some, or many?
- Do any other orthodox theologians or movements propound this view?

We can think of the authority of tradition in terms of concentric circles. At the center is Scripture, followed by creeds, confessions, and doctors, with other teachers comprising the outermost circle (see fig. 4.2).[49] They are all authoritative, but their authority is felt in different ways. The forms of tradition lying closer to the center are more certain and normative. So, theologians have greater freedom with respect to traditions that are further from the center. Careful assessments of theological proposals will begin in the center and work out, so to speak, seeking to discern if and how a theology interacts with the various forms of tradition. This range of interactions is the topic of the next principle.

3. *Discern the theology's "genre."* Earlier we discussed five ways theologians consciously engage with the tradition. To read critically and charitably we must identify which genre a theology is displaying,

49. Though I develop it differently, I borrow the idea of concentric circles from Robert E. Webber, "An Evangelical and Catholic Methodology," in *The Use of the Bible in Theology/Evangelical Options*, ed. Robert K. Johnston (Eugene, OR: Wipf and Stock, 1997), 146–47.

Figure 4.2

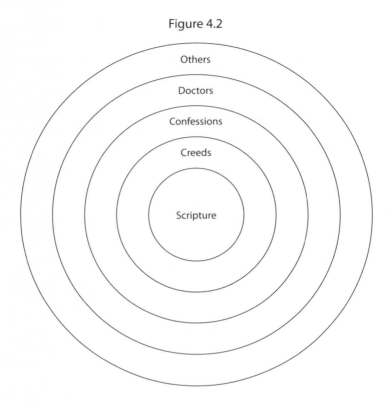

and knowing a few markers will help toward that end. Such markers include the following:

- The *language* adopted by the theology is one key marker to help discern its type. Traditional or biblical language will more often be on display in celebratory and conservative approaches. Philosophical language or language from another domain is often present in the other three genres.
- *Biblical references* and allusions will be more obvious in the celebratory and conservative modes and less so as you move from constructive to critical to contradictory.
- The *ends* for which the arguments are being made differ as you move from one type to another. Celebratory theology aims

to exult, conservative to rearticulate, constructive to answer broader questions, critical to revise, and contradictory to reject. In the end, repeated exposure to a variety of theologies is the best way to develop the skill of discerning types.

The ability to discern theological genres aids us in a number of ways. First, our expectations will be properly shaped so that we do not impose on a text a standard it cannot meet. Knowing the genre helps us to be sensitive to why the author did not say more than she did. For example, one cannot expect a critical work to do what a conservative work does, and vice versa, since one seeks to preserve while the other seeks to challenge. As in other areas of life, inappropriate expectations only lead to disappointment.

Second, it helps us understand why the author appears to be saying too much. For example, theologians writing in the constructive genre often take one theological idea or hint and expand imaginatively about the potential ecclesial and cultural implications of this theological nugget. The biblical teachings that God is love and that God is three persons have been extended to address questions of church, marriage, even the demise of Western civilization.[50] Some of these explorations may be a stretch, but to some degree that is their aim—to stretch theology beyond its traditional interests.

Finally, discerning the genre helps us determine the right criteria for assessment. For instance, one might evaluate a conservative work on the basis of how faithful a rendition of the tradition it represents. However, that criterion would be less appropriate (though not irrelevant) for a more critical theology, whose evaluation might more closely be tied to its rationality and overall fidelity to Scripture (as complicated as it might be to separate these sources). Along these lines, one might assess a constructive piece on the basis of whether it is a plausible expansion—in light of Scripture and tradition—of a traditional theme on the accuracy of its representation of the tradition and its ability to evoke worship.

4. *Know how arguments are constructed in relation to tradition.* Closely related to the issue of genre is the issue of how arguments

---

50. On the latter, see Colin E. Gunton, *The One, the Three and the Many: God, Creation and the Culture of Modernity* (Cambridge: Cambridge University Press, 1993).

are actually made with respect to tradition. Certain genres tend to adopt certain modes of argument more often. John Frame outlines three common types of arguments related to tradition used by contemporary theologians:

- *Identification*: the theologian chooses a historical or contemporary movement to inhabit and endorse, allowing it to set the standards of truth. For example, one might adopt liberation or dispensational theology as the lens through which all else is evaluated.
- *Antithesis*: the theologian chooses a historical movement or theologian to oppose as a paradigmatic case of error. For instance, it is fairly common to see this done with Hellenistic, medieval Catholic, or fundamentalist theologies.
- *Triangulation*: the theologian spotlights two or more interesting and respectable historical movements, identifies weaknesses in them, and provides a synthesis or middle way that resolves or overcomes those weaknesses. For example, some might see Barth as the synthesis of evangelical and liberal theologies, providing a middle way between two extremes with respect to the doctrine of Scripture.[51]

When we become familiar with these types of arguments, we will be more alert to the tradition from which the theologian argues, be better able to identify the genre, and be able to thoughtfully and sympathetically engage the doctrine from within the assumptions and limits set by its chosen method of argumentation. In short, we become readers who are better able to engage theologies from within two worlds—our own and the author's.

Conclusion: Staying True to the Past

The Christian past is not something to be ignored, nor is it something to which we are doomed. Rather, the Christian past shapes and must shape the present way we think about our faith. Theologians must

---

51. Frame, *Doctrine of the Word of God*, 602–3.

be conversant with past voices—creeds, confessions, doctors, and other theologians—if they are to stay true to the gospel. Granted, theologians interact differently with the Christian tradition at different times, yet most see this interaction as part of faithfully carrying out their vocation. Thus as we engage doctrine critically, we cannot sidestep the question of a theology's fidelity to the Christian tradition. Some sensitivity is required since, as Lints notes, "consensus among theologians ought not to be a criterion of adequacy in theology, nor ought the lack of consensus to be a criterion of inadequacy."[52] Along similar lines, theological novelty does not equate with error, nor does antiquity equal truthfulness. Yet if a theology has been held "nowhere, ever, by anyone"—the opposite of Vincent's canon—we have every reason to question it. Truth is a historical category, not just a philosophical one. Theology must, therefore, be true to its tradition, and not only to Scripture, since it is through the former that our faithfulness to the latter will be secured.

52. Lints, *Fabric of Theology*, 98. In principle we must agree with Lints although consensus is a serious consideration and cannot be discounted.

5

Believing Possible Things

Theology and Reason

Faith and reason are like two wings on which the human
spirit rises to the contemplation of truth.

—John Paul II, *Fides et Ratio*

I've believed as many as six impossible things before
breakfast.

—White Queen, *Through the Looking-Glass,
and What Alice Found There*

In the fifth chapter of *Through the Looking Glass*, Alice encounters
the White Queen, who looks disheveled and out of sorts. Compassionate child that she is, Alice proceeds to help the queen pull herself
together—putting on her shawl, adjusting a brooch, and brushing and
styling the queen's hair. After finishing Alice exclaims, "Come, you look
rather better now! . . . But really you should have a lady's-maid!" To
this the queen replies, "I'm sure I'll take you with pleasure! Twopence
a week, and jam every other day." The following conversation ensues:

121

Alice: I don't want you to hire *me*—and I don't care for jam.

Queen: It's very good jam.

Alice: Well, I don't want any *to-day*, at any rate.

Queen: You couldn't have it if you *did* want it. The rule is, jam to-morrow and jam yesterday—but never jam to-day.

Alice: It must come sometimes to "jam to-day."

Queen: No, it can't. It's jam every other day: to-day isn't any other day, you know.

Alice: I don't understand you. It's dreadfully confusing!

The queen then attempts to demystify this conversation, quipping, "That's the effect of living backwards. It always makes one a little giddy at first—"

Alice: Living backwards! I never heard of such a thing!

Queen: But there's one great advantage in it, that one's memory works both ways.

Alice: I'm sure mine only works one way. I can't remember things before they happen.

Queen: It's a poor sort of memory that only works backwardly.

Alice: What sort of things do you remember best?

Queen: Oh, things that happened the week after next. For instance, now there's the King's Messenger. He's in prison now, being punished: and the trial doesn't even begin till next Wednesday: and of course the crime comes last of all.

Alice, confused again but knowing something is awry, finally responds, "There's a mistake somewhere—." As their conversation comes to a close, the queen asks Alice her age:

Alice: I'm seven and a half exactly.

Queen: You needn't say "exactually." I can believe it without that. Now I'll give *you* something to believe. I'm just one hundred and one, five months and a day.

Alice: I can't believe *that*!

Queen: Can't you? Try again: draw a long breath, and shut your eyes.

As if summing up their entire interaction, a laughing Alice retorts, "There's no use trying, one *can't* believe impossible things." To this the queen concludes, "I dare say you haven't had much practice. When I was your age, I always did it for half an hour a day. Why, sometimes I've believed as many as six impossible things before breakfast."[1]

Indeed, these three dialogues are all about getting Alice to believe impossible—or irrational—things. And try as she may, she cannot bring herself to do so. Alice is a rational creature, even at age seven. The perplexity and frustration she feels in conversation with the queen results from the tenacious irrationality of her interlocutor. What Alice quickly discerns, and what most of us know by experience, is that conversations, relationships, and life generally do not go well when people choose to be irrational.

* * * * *

Christian theology is not exempt from the demand to be rational. Some would contend that Christianity requires that we abandon reason and "believe impossible things." And while it is true that we are summoned to believe incredible, unfathomable (though not impossible) things, we are not at the same time called to forsake rationality. Some of us, in fact, do need to heed the White Queen's counsel and get some practice in believing, but many of us need to apply our minds more exactly to the truths of the faith. Christian theology concerns truth, which according to McGrath has three dimensions relevant to Christian doctrine. First, the Greek *alētheia* involves discovering the way things are in reality. Second, the Latin *veritas* concerns the exactness or precision of an utterance, usually having to do with the past. It deals with the accurate narration of past events. Third, the Hebrew *emunah* refers to truth in the sense of trust or trustworthiness and has an implicit future reference.[2]

1. Lewis Carroll, *The Best of Lewis Carroll*, reissue ed. (Secaucus, NJ: Castle, 2011), 220–25.
2. Alister E. McGrath, *The Genesis of Doctrine: A Study in the Foundation of Doctrinal Criticism* (Grand Rapids: Eerdmans, 1997), 73–77.

Theologians must be concerned with all three conceptions of truth as they seek to faithfully explicate the revelation of God, the gospel, and the implications of both for creation. Theology is not solely about trusting God without any concern for precision in our understanding and articulation of who God is. John Wesley, speaking of the importance of reason to Christianity, writes, "It is a fundamental principle with us that to renounce reason is to renounce religion, that religion and reason go hand in hand, and that all irrational religion is false religion."[3]

In the previous chapters, we examined the ways theology can be biblical and traditional. In this chapter, we will explore how theology is and must be rational. We will first examine the controverted relationship between faith and reason, or theology and philosophy, on our way to defining our use of the term "reason." Second, we will examine the effects of the fall and redemption on reason and what ramifications these have for how we employ reason in theology. Third, we will enumerate the uses of reason in theology as they have been understood historically. Fourth, we will establish standards of rationality, or conditions theology must meet if it is to make a claim for being rational. Finally, the chapter will close by drawing out guiding principles for assessing the rationality of theological proposals. As stated in the previous chapters, these issues are complicated, but this chapter will provide a good starting point for understanding the role of reason in theology.

Faith and Reason

To some degree, the history of Christian theology has been governed by the sentiment of a famous saying of Tertullian's:

> What indeed has Athens to do with Jerusalem? What concord is there between the Academy and the Church? What between heretics and Christians? Our instruction comes from "the porch of Solomon," who had himself taught that "the Lord should be sought in simplicity of heart."

3. John Wesley "Letter to Rutherford," quoted in Don Thorsen, *The Wesleyan Quadrilateral: Scripture, Tradition, Reason and Experience as a Model of Evangelical Theology* (Lexington: Emeth, 2005), 107.

Away with all attempts to produce a mottled Christianity of Stoic, Platonic, and dialectic composition! We want no curious disputation after possessing Christ Jesus, no inquisition after enjoying the gospel![4]

What relationship is there between philosophy and theology, between the "religion" of the philosophers and that of Christ? The curiosity of the philosophers is, to some degree, antithetical to the gospel, so that there should be no such thing as "Platonic Christians." To Tertullian, philosophers are the "patriarchs of heretics."[5] While these statements may seem bombastic and severe, they express well the question of the relationship reason is to have to the faith.[6] Our answer to the question largely depends on how we define philosophy. For instance, philosophy can refer to (1) a person's worldview; (2) the academic discipline involving metaphysics, epistemology, ethics, logic, and so on, which employs specific concepts and tools; and (3) a commitment to clear, analytical thinking.[7] Tertullian's statement seems directed toward something like the first and second definitions, rather than the third. He rejects philosophy as the adoption and use of concepts foreign to the Christian faith, not derived from divine revelation, and viewed as a preparation for the gospel. However, his view is only one in a range of historical perspectives on the relationship between Jerusalem and Athens. Kevin Vanhoozer helpfully groups the various ways the two disciplines have related into five categories, under the rubric of Christ (theology) versus concept (philosophy):

1. *Christ subsumed under concept:* All talk about God *must* use the language and concepts of Athens (philosophy) if it wants

4. Tertullian, *Prescription Against Heretics* 7, in *Ante-Nicene Fathers*, 10 vols., ed. Philip Schaff et al., vol. 3, *Latin Christianity: Its Founder, Tertullian* (Buffalo: Christian Literature, 1885).

5. Tertullian, *De Anima* 3, in *Ante-Nicene Christian Library*, 24 vols., ed. Alexander Roberts and Sir James Donaldson, *The Writings of Tertullian, Vol. 2* (Edinburgh: T&T Clark, 1870), 15:416.

6. Although the issues surrounding theology and philosophy are not identical with those concerning faith and reason, they are very closely related.

7. David K. Clark, *To Know and Love God: Method for Theology*, Foundations of Evangelical Theology (Wheaton: Crossway, 2003), 296–300. Clark also includes the analytical study of another discipline, such as the philosophy of science, as another way we define the term.

to count as rational, intelligible discourse. Kant and Hegel are prime examples of this view.

2. *Christ grounded in concept:* While not subsuming theology into philosophy, the latter serves as the foundation of theology's speech about God. The early Christian apologists, Clement of Alexandria, and modern theologians Paul Tillich and David Tracy are representatives of this view.

3. *Christ in dialogue with concept:* Neither discipline governs the other, but each maintains authority relative to its respective spheres of academy (philosophy) and church (theology). The two may coincide from time to time, and there is a desire to correlate the language of philosophy with that of theology, but no attempt is made to subsume the latter under the former. Aquinas, Schleiermacher, and Bultmann are representatives of this perspective.

4. *Christ the Lord of concept:* In this view, philosophy becomes the servant of theology. Theology operates independently of philosophy and only uses philosophical concepts from time to time if they help explicate the logic of the gospel. Theology is under no obligation to commit to some conceptual scheme. Anselm and Barth are exemplars of this view.

5. *Christ the contradiction of concept:* Theology and philosophy should have nothing to do with each other because they speak such different languages and have such different starting points and aims. Theology is the speech of the community of faith; it is specifically the church's language. This makes it immune to criticism from the outside. Only those within the community are able to check its speech about God against its own norms, rather than be subjected to foreign standards of truth and rationality. Tertullian and Luther are theologians associated with this viewpoint.[8]

While holders of each viewpoint value precision in thought and speech, they differ slightly in how they use the term "philosophy"

8. Kevin J. Vanhoozer, "Christ and Concept: Doing Theology and the 'Ministry' of Philosophy," in *Doing Theology in Today's World: Essays in Honor of Kenneth S. Kantzer*, ed. John D. Woodbridge (Grand Rapids: Zondervan, 1994), 111–28.

and in their relative optimism regarding its usefulness to theology. Some tend to view philosophy as a worldview or orientation that is opposed to or inconsistent with theology, while others view it as a worldview that overlaps significantly with the Christian faith. Meanwhile, some view philosophy more as an academic discipline with its own vocabulary, conceptual frameworks, and standards of rationality that are foreign to the faith, while others see these features as gifts for articulating the faith.

How we answer the problem of faith and reason largely turns on how we conceive of the theology-philosophy relationship and how we define the terms involved. As a matter of fact, even "reason" is often an ambiguous term in these conversations. It can be defined as (1) the ability to think about anything, or the faculty by which we come to know things; (2) the ability to think analytically and precisely about certain things, as when we apply the rules of logic; (3) natural knowledge presented to or impressed upon the mind; (4) an intellectual discipline involving formal ways of analyzing and arguing from these naturally known principles; and (5) human thinking done independently of God in a self-conscious manner.[9] John Hildrop calls reason "that much perverted and abused word . . . the Abuse of which has been and continues to be, as fatal to the Interests of Religion . . . as any Error in Language can be supposed to be."[10] Therefore, for clarity's sake, we will define reason as *the human faculty by which we come to know things and by which we think carefully and analytically about reality*. Yet even when understood in this fairly neutral manner, we must still wrestle with the question of whether reason has any limits with respect to Christian theology. If so, what are they, particularly in light of the creation, fall, redemption, and

9. Definitions drawn from Clark, *To Know and Love God*, 299–300; Francis Turretin, *Institutes of Elenctic Theology*, ed. James T. Dennison Jr., trans. George Musgrave Giger, vol. 1 (Phillipsburg, NJ: P&R, 1992), 23–24; Richard A. Muller, *Post-Reformation Reformed Dogmatics*, vol. 2, *Holy Scripture: The Cognitive Foundation of Theology*, 2nd ed. (Grand Rapids: Baker Academic, 2003), 388–89.

10. John Hildrop, *Reflections upon Reason*, taken from David A. Pailin, "Reason in Relation to Scripture and Tradition," in *Scripture, Tradition and Reason: A Study in the Criteria of Christian Doctrine*, ed. Richard J. Bauckham and Benjamin Drewery (Edinburgh: T&T Clark, 1988), 219.

consummation of humanity and all its faculties? This is an important matter that has occupied theologians for generations, and it is
worthwhile to pause for a moment to reflect on it before proceeding
to more practical concerns.

Reason from Creation to Consummation

As an aspect of human personhood, reason is not exempt from the
divine drama within which all people find themselves. In fact, our
descriptions of reason are incorrect insofar as they do not have God
the Creator and Redeemer as their primary reference point. Reason must be understood according to the drama of creation, fall,
redemption, and consummation, a drama within which God is the
main character. How do we understand reason in relation to these
various acts of the drama?

First, *reason is created*. John Webster writes, "The creator en-
dows creatures with reason in order that, hearing his intelligible
word of promise and command, they may know him, and so love
and obey him."[11] Three things stand out from Webster's statement.
The first is that created reason is good by virtue of its origin and
purpose, being from God and for God. The second is that created
reason is contingent; it is dependent on God for its continued life
and proper functioning. The third is that reason shares in the finitude and limitedness of all creaturely reality. Thus at the creation,
reason functioned properly, even if immaturely, by submitting to
God, thinking rightly about him, and acquiescing to the bounds
set by its Maker.

Second, *reason is fallen*. "Reasoning," Vanhoozer writes, "is something that people do, and like any instrument, it is only as reliable as
the person wielding it."[12] Reason undergoes the corruption inherent
in all human life post–Genesis 3. Rather than reason being used to
acknowledge and submit to God, it is used to deny God and gain

11. John Webster, *The Domain of the Word: Scripture and Theological Reason*
(London: Bloomsbury T&T Clark, 2013), 124.
12. Kevin J. Vanhoozer, *The Drama of Doctrine: A Canonical-Linguistic Approach
to Christian Theology* (Louisville: Westminster John Knox, 2005), 301–2.

power over others.[13] Fallen reason is blinded, Turretin observes, with respect to the law and gospel.[14] It desires to throw off the shackles of contingency and finitude and become an autonomous, self-sufficient principle, having what one author calls the presumptions of aseity and universality.[15] This does not entail that reason is altogether null and void and incapable of any good, even in its fallen state. Instead, Webster aptly concludes, "Embroiled in the creature's bid for freedom from the creator, reason loses its orientation to its proper end, and so compromises its goodness. It becomes 'pure' reason, reason on its own; and precisely this is its corruption."[16] Fallen reason is not the way it's supposed to be.

Third, *reason can be redeemed*. In the same way that God does not abandon creation but redeems it through Christ, created and fallen reason is not forsaken. "The renewal of creation has been wrought by the Self-same Word Who made it in the beginning," writes Athanasius.[17] Scripture speaks of the renewal of the mind (Rom. 12:2), the bringing into being of a new creature (2 Cor. 5:17). The cross liberates human reason to be restored to the image of divine reason. Restored reason is rightly oriented reason: it takes its proper place in the economy of God's gracious work by depending on God, submitting to his rule, and seeing love toward him as its ultimate end. Restored reason is not perfected reason; rather, it is "sound and healed by grace" as part of the whole person.[18]

Finally, *reason will be perfected*. The fact that created and redeemed reason remains unperfected reason directs our attention to the eschaton. It is only then that reason, while still good, contingent, and limited, will function as it should. It will be resurrected reason: powerful, glorious, virtuous. Those who have this hope properly esteem reason, neither underrating nor overrating it.

13. Vanhoozer, *Drama of Doctrine*, 302.
14. Turretin, *Institutes*, 1:24.
15. Ernstpeter Maurer, "The Perplexity and Complexity of Sinful and Redeemed Reason," in *Reason and the Reasons of Faith*, ed. Paul J. Griffiths and Reinhard Hütter (London: T&T Clark, 2005), 209–10.
16. Webster, *Domain of the Word*, 125.
17. Athanasius, *On the Incarnation* (Yonkers, NY: St. Vladimir's Seminary Press, 2002), 26.
18. Phrase borrowed from Turretin, *Institutes*, 1:31.

Not only is our knowledge of *God* fragmentary, all our knowledge is. Yet we do not adopt the attitude that all reasoning is futile or take the posture of epistemic sloth. Reason even in its brokenness is a gift of God by which we come to know the Maker and the world he has made. Reason can be trusted, even if not worshiped. It is a minister of God's truth, not its master.[19] And when operating with due patience and humility, created, fallen, and redeemed reason occupies an important place in the work of theology.

The Uses of Reason in Theology

The relationship between reason and faith is complicated. Complications notwithstanding, theologians have gone a long way to show not only the usefulness of reason but also its necessity to theology. Calvin, for example, notes that it was the "diligent inquisition" into the truth of Paul's teaching for which Luke commends the Bereans (Acts 17:11).[20] Aquinas, responding to the question "Whether sacred doctrine is a matter of argument?" offers Titus 1:9: "[An overseer] must hold firmly to the trustworthy message as it has been taught, so that he can encourage others by sound doctrine and refute those who oppose it." An overseer is called to employ reason in answering objections to the faith and in making the faith clear. Aquinas adds:

> But sacred doctrine makes use even of human reason, not, indeed, to prove faith (for thereby the merit of faith would come to an end), but to make clear other things that are put forward in this doctrine. Since therefore grace does not destroy nature but perfects it, natural reason should minister to faith as the natural bent of the will ministers to charity. Hence the Apostle says: "Bringing into captivity every understanding unto the obedience of Christ" (2 Cor. 10:5).[21]

19. Turretin differentiates between what he calls the despotic use of reason and the ministerial use. Turretin, *Institutes*, 1:25.

20. John Calvin, *Calvin's Commentaries*, vol. 19, *Acts 14–28 and Romans 1–16*, ed. Henry Beveridge (Grand Rapids: Baker, 2003), 141.

21. Thomas Aquinas, *The "Summa Theologiae" of St. Thomas Aquinas: Latin-English Edition, Prima Pars, Q. 1–64*, trans. Fathers of the English Dominican Province (Scotts Valley, CA: CreateSpace, 2009), Q. 1, a. 8.

The use of reason, according to these theologians, has biblical precedent.[22] Beyond these brief examples, what are the legitimate uses of reason in the work of theological formulation? At least the following must be included:

- To track down the theological material within the Scriptures
- To illustrate or provide concepts that help to explain the truths of revelation
- To elucidate and draw out the implications and consequences of truths handed down from Scripture and tradition (through a process of logical analysis and inference)
- To gather the material of revelation into one system that expresses the unity of truth
- To reconcile apparent conflicts within Scripture or between the contents of Scripture and tradition
- To ensure consistency of doctrines being simultaneously affirmed
- To show what truths can be ascertained without the aid of divine revelation
- To show what truths can be attained only through divine revelation
- To address issues not commanded or forbidden by Scripture or tradition
- To support orthodoxy and combat heterodoxy through sound argumentation[23]

Whether consciously or not, theologians are always leaning on reason in order to do their work responsibly. To theologize responsibly requires that one be rational, and to be rational implies that certain standards of rationality must be met. What might these standards be?

---

22. See Muller, *Post-Reformation Reformed Dogmatics*, vol. 1, *Prolegomena to Theology*, 2nd ed. (Grand Rapids: Baker Academic, 2003), 399, for more on this.

23. See Pailin, "Reason," 217; Thorsen, *Wesleyan Quadrilateral*, 110; Turretin, *Institutes*, 1:24; Webster, *Domain of the Word*, 130–31; Muller, *Post-Reformation Reformed Dogmatics*, 1:400; Herman Bavinck, *Reformed Dogmatics*, vol. 1, *Prolegomena*, ed. John Bolt, trans. John Vriend (Grand Rapids: Baker Academic, 2003), 617–18.

The Rationality of Theology

While the lists differ slightly from author to author, many thinkers seem to agree that all sound reasoning must at least adhere to
the three "Cs": coherence, consistency, and cogency. Theology is no
different. While my use of these terms may not be philosophically
precise, I will use them as a way of grouping the various standards
of rationality that theology must meet.

Coherence

The coherence of an argument involves the quality of its logic.
Generally speaking, logical arguments fall into two categories: deductive and inductive. A *deductive argument* is one in which the premises
guarantee the truth of the conclusion; that is, if the premises are true,
then the conclusion must be true. An *inductive argument* is one in
which the premises make the conclusion more or less probable; the
premises provide grounds or support for the conclusion.[24] Let's take
a look at these arguments in more detail.

DEDUCTIVE ARGUMENTS

These often take the form of syllogisms, which are arguments
consisting of two premises and one conclusion. There are several
types of syllogisms, but for the sake of brevity we will consider
two common types in theology. Knowing these (and other types)
will help you form a basis for logical analysis of any conclusion,
theological or otherwise. First we will examine a *modus ponens*
argument:

> If P, then Q
> P
> Therefore, Q

For example, one could argue:

24. These definitions and much of the following discussion are drawn from J. P.
Moreland, *Love Your God with All Your Mind: The Role of Reason in the Life of
the Soul*, 2nd ed. (Colorado Springs: NavPress, 2012), 130–41.

If you believe in Jesus (P), then you are saved (Q).

You believe in Jesus. (P)

Therefore, you are saved.

If, however, one argued,

If you believe in Jesus (P), then you are saved (Q);

you are saved (Q);

therefore, you believe in Jesus,

this would be false because the conclusion is not supported by the premises.[25] In the Reformation debates concerning the presence of Christ at the Lord's Supper, the Reformed used this type of syllogism to refute their opponents who argued for the real presence of Christ at the Eucharist. The syllogism is simple:

If Christ's body is truly human (P), then it cannot be everywhere (Q).

Christ's body is truly human (P).

Therefore, it cannot be everywhere (Q).

Therefore, in the context of this argument, it cannot be held that Christ is really or physically present at the celebration of the Lord's Supper, since Scripture tells us that his body is real, and if it is real, then it is circumscribed to certain spaces.[26]

A *demonstrative* syllogism describes another type of argument common in theological discussions. It is defined as a syllogism that produces knowledge on the basis of necessary premises and the most

---

25. A second, similar and common type of argument is the *modus tollens*:

If P, then Q

Not Q

Therefore, not P

For example, one could argue: If naturalistic evolution were true (P), then human beings would simply be physical systems (Q); human beings are not merely physical systems, in that they have souls (not Q); therefore, naturalistic evolution is not true (not P).

26. Example is taken from Turretin, *Institutes*, 1:27.

certain reasons for the conclusion.[27] The structure of the argument is as follows:

> Major premise (A)
>
> Minor premise (B)
>
> Therefore, conclusion (C)

In a discussion of Christ's human nature, Aquinas asks whether Jesus had any knowledge acquired through sense experience. In responding, Aquinas uses a chain of demonstrative syllogisms, where each conclusion forms the next major premise (I use this example to illustrate, so do not worry about the details):

Major premise: nothing that was planted in human nature was lacking in the nature assumed by the Word. (A)

Minor premise: it is clear that God planted in human nature both an active intellect (one that acts to draw conceptual knowledge from sense experience) and a passive intellect (a soul that receives the form of things perceived). (B)

Conclusion: the soul of Christ had an active intellect. (C)

New major premise: the soul of Christ had an active intellect. (A)

Minor premise: God and nature make nothing that does not possess a proper function. (B)

Conclusion: the active intellect of Christ had its proper function. (C)

New major premise: the active intellect of Christ had its proper function. (A)

Minor premise: the proper function of the active intellect is to acquire knowledge from sense experience. (B)

Conclusion: Christ acquired knowledge through sense experience. (C)[28]

---

27. Norman Kretzmann, ed. and trans., *William of Sherwood's "Introduction to Logic"* (Minneapolis: University of Minnesota Press, 1966), 69.

28. Frederick Christian Bauerschmidt, *Thomas Aquinas: Faith, Reason, and Following Christ* (Oxford: Oxford University Press, 2013), 152–53. Original discussion is found in Aquinas, *Summa Theologiae* IIIa, Q. 9, a. 4.

In the first syllogism, the major premise is drawn from Scripture and the theological tradition, while the minor premise is taken from Aristotle's account of the soul. The conclusion is drawn from two necessary premises. This conclusion then forms the major premise of the second syllogism, with Aristotle providing the minor premise. The same pattern follows in the third syllogism. Sometimes arguments will begin with a general axiom (derived from reason) as the major premise, while something derived from Scripture and tradition provides the minor.[29] These are all what might be called mixed syllogisms, and they are common in the tradition.[30] I offer these very brief examples to make the point that knowing how these arguments are constructed and being able to detect them is helpful in assessing the rationality of a theological proposal. Sound logic, or a coherent argument, must have both sound premises and a sound conclusion, and we must grow in being able to discern these as we read various theological arguments. I will discuss these principles further in the final section of this chapter.

INDUCTIVE ARGUMENTS

A good inductive argument, remember, is one in which the premises make the conclusion more probable than other explanations. One fruitful approach to such arguments is called *inference to the best explanation*. In this approach, we have certain data or phenomena to explain. The goal is to provide the hypothesis (or theory) that best accounts for the data. The criteria for such an explanation include (but are not limited to) the following:[31]

1. *Explanatory scope*: the best hypothesis will explain a wider range of data than competing explanations/theories. This refers to *how much* data can be explained by the theory.

2. *Explanatory power*: the best theory will make the observable data more epistemically probable than its competitors. This refers to *how well* the available data is explained.

---

29. Bauerschmidt, *Thomas Aquinas*, 153.
30. See Turretin, *Institutes*, 1:26–27.
31. This discussion is taken from J. P. Moreland and William Lane Craig, *Philosophical Foundations for a Christian Worldview* (Downers Grove, IL: IVP Academic, 2003), 61–62.

3. *Plausibility*: the best hypothesis will be implied by a greater *variety* of accepted/established truths.

4. *Accord with accepted beliefs*: the best theory, when joined with accepted truths, will imply fewer falsehoods than competing theories.

5. *Comparative superiority*: the best hypothesis betters its rivals in meeting criteria 1–4, indicating that its probability is higher than the competition.

One can see how these arguments would be common (even the most common) in theological discussions in which we are often trying to provide the best explanation of the biblical "data" (not the best description, to be sure), and to do so in accordance with accepted beliefs (the tradition or otherwise). Theological proposals are almost always trying to reason to the best explanation of Scripture. The Formula of Chalcedon, for example, reasons on the basis of Scripture (e.g., those speaking of Jesus as "like us in every way" or "growing in wisdom and stature") and accepted truths (e.g., that Jesus is divine as found in the Nicene Creed) that Jesus somehow exists as a single person with two undivided but unmixed natures. Many other arguments have the same form. A theologian asks what the whole counsel of Scripture teaches and forms the hypothesis that best explains all the phenomena of Scripture. While theologians seek to provide the most probable explanation and their arguments are therefore provisional, the arguments are aimed at the highest likelihood of truth.

Consistency

According to John Webster, having a theological system "is rendered necessary by the comprehensiveness and singularity of the object of Christian confession and praise."[32] The unity of truth is guaranteed by the one God whose actions we explicate in the work of theology. It is theology's task, as Herman Bavinck observes, to "gather up the material of revelation into one system that expresses the unity of truth." He adds, "Theology does not rest until it has discovered

---

32. Webster, *Domain of the Word*, 144.

the unity underlying revelation."[33] Talk of unity implies a system in which each of its parts is in its proper place and does not contradict or detract from another part. In a system all parts hang together in one way or another, and a test of the quality of a proposal is how well its parts do this. We can refer to this as *systematic consistency*. Theology is concerned not solely with treating individual doctrines in isolation but also with seeing how one impinges on another. How does A relate to B, C, and D? If I relate A to D in this way, does that negate B and force me to alter C?[34] For example, a doctrine of creation clearly interacts with the doctrines of God, sin, and eschatology, as the diagram below illustrates.[35]

Figure 5.1

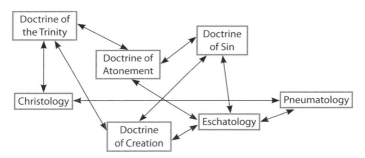

One doctrine cannot be described accurately without reference to the others, and one can misconstrue a doctrine because sufficient attention has not been paid to related doctrines. Heresies are sometimes the offspring of systematic inconsistency. Schleiermacher contends that the ancient christological heresies resulted from inconsistency among the doctrines of Christ, salvation, and humanity. He notes that while the ancient heresies accepted the basic Christian belief that salvation is accomplished by Jesus Christ, their understanding of human nature and of Christ renders that belief inconsistent. Put

33. Bavinck, *Reformed Dogmatics*, 1:618.

34. Stephen Williams, "Observations on the Future of System," in *Always Reforming: Explorations in Systematic Theology*, ed. A. T. B. McGowan (Downers Grove, IL: IVP Academic, 2006), 49.

35. See the brief discussion in Nancey C. Murphy, *Reasoning and Rhetoric in Religion* (Valley Forge, PA: Trinity Press International, 1994), 198–99.

differently, given the kinds of anthropologies and Christologies they propound, they cannot consistently hold that Jesus brings salvation to the world. For example, if Jesus is merely a human being like the rest of us (i.e., Ebionite heresy), then he cannot redeem since he is in need of the same redemption that we require. In this case, the doctrine of salvation puts pressure on Christology, so that the latter has to make sense of the former. Soteriology checks (but also enriches) Christology.[36] In contemporary theology, discussions about trinitarian theology, as another example, are often concerned with how the doctrine of the Trinity informs or has not sufficiently informed other areas such as ecclesiology, anthropology, and so forth.[37] Although not necessarily framed this way, these are conversations about systematic consistency.

Cogency

Cogency refers to whether an argument is convincing or not. Under the rubric of cogency, we will explore some logical and rational fallacies to which theologians are not immune. Each of these fallacies is problematic, not because of the content of what is believed but because of a defect in the argument. Let us look at six such fallacies.[38]

Appeal to pity. In this fallacy, the premises of the argument are logically irrelevant to the conclusion. Instead, the premises are emotionally moving, so that the conclusion *seems* to follow naturally. These arguments are persuasive because they are able to evoke sympathy from the reader in favor of an argument, even if the argument itself is not logically persuasive. For example, one might argue, "We cannot hold to male-only ordination since it is so oppressive to women. Therefore, we must allow for equality in ordination." The argument's strength largely rests in the emotions it evokes rather than the strength of its premises.

Ad hominem argument. This fallacy occurs when a writer argues against another's position by attacking the person rather than

---

36. See discussion in McGrath, *Genesis of Doctrine*, 77–78. See Friedrich Schleiermacher, *The Christian Faith*, ed. H. R. Mackintosh and J. S. Stewart (London: T&T Clark, 1999), 97–101.

37. See, e.g., Colin E. Gunton, *Father, Son and Holy Spirit: Toward a Fully Trinitarian Theology* (London: T&T Clark, 2003).

38. Taken from Moreland, *Love Your God*, 137–41.

dismantling the argument. For example, one might say, "His argument against black theology is rubbish because he's white, privileged, and has an agenda, so he cannot possibly understand the issues." While that may be partially true, it is by no means a sound argument against the man's views. This argument seeks to discredit the person rather than the ideas and argument put forward.

Appeal to the people. In one form of this fallacy, the writer appeals to the "established conclusions" of some group or to the authority of some respected group as grounds for the conclusion. The argument goes something like this: Since this revered group (and anyone respectable) believes this is true, then it must be true and accepted. For example, one could argue that since "most theologians" believe that revelation is personal rather than propositional, revelation is therefore personal, and theologies assuming propositional revelation need to be rethought. While that may or may not be the case, the argument largely rests on the fact that "most theologians" hold a certain belief.

Genetic fallacy. The perpetrator of this fallacy confuses the origin of the idea with reasons for the idea and rejects the idea because of its origin and not because of the lack of grounds for it. You see this kind of argument in theology when a concept drawn from Greek philosophy is used to explain the deity of Christ or the hypostatic union. Some fault the theology of Nicaea or Chalcedon because the roots of their conceptualities are "foreign" to primitive Christianity and therefore pollute its pure message.

Straw man. Another common fallacy occurs when a writer distorts the position of another so that it is the worst possible version of her view. The writer then refutes the caricatured view and concludes that the original position had no merit and was soundly defeated. A simple example: "Every thing needs a cause; God is a thing; therefore, God needs a cause." The weakness of this kind of argument should be obvious.

Begging the question. This fallacy involves taking the conclusion one is trying to prove as one of the premises used to prove that conclusion. A subtle form of it occurs when we formulate an argument that assumes the conclusion rather than establishing it. For example, one could argue: (1) Either God exists or the moon is made of green cheese; (2) the moon is not made of green cheese; (3) therefore, God exists. While the argument is a logically valid one, it is not convincing since the only reason anyone would accept it is if they already believe the conclusion.[39]

Much more could be said about fallacies, but I offer these as ones commonly encountered in theology, in popular and sometimes academic venues. As we read theology, we should be aware of when we or others commit these fallacies. Theology cannot avoid the requirement to be cogent, coherent, and consistent. Our subject matter demands that we not take a flight from reason and assume we are doing God or faith a service. Having some *basic* knowledge of logic, understanding the interconnectedness of doctrine, and being attuned to fallacies can go some way in helping us read theology critically and even charitably.

Theology on the Dock: Some Guiding Principles

The chief burden of this chapter has been to increase awareness of issues related to the place of reason in theological discourse, to highlight how reason has been used in theology throughout history, and to provide examples of the kinds of rational tests theology must pass to be deemed rational. For those who feel overwhelmed by the details, I would like (as I've done in previous chapters) to sum up this chapter by providing principles to guide the assessing of theology in relation to reason. These will come in the form of questions to be posed about every theological proposal.

1. *Is it coherent and convincing?* In a scene from *Alice in Wonderland*, the March Hare counsels Alice to say what she means. She responds, "I do, at least—at least I mean what I say—that's the same thing you know." The Hatter disagrees, protesting that such logic is as silly as claiming that "I see what I eat" is the same thing as "I eat what I see."[40] Reasoning breaks down even in the simplest conversations. As students of theology, we must apply whatever rules of logic we know and be aware of common fallacies in order to engage the proposal responsibly. But with time and practice, flaws in reasoning like Alice's are more ably exposed. Moreover, we must remember that

---

39. Moreland and Craig, *Philosophical Foundations*, 57.
40. Carroll, *Best of Lewis Carroll*, 60.

many theological proposals will be inductive in nature, seeking to offer the best theory or explanation of a particular Christian teaching. But the use of the adjective "best" connotes that our knowledge is limited and thus our theories are provisional. Thus charity and humility become important as we engage doctrine.

2. *Is it systematically consistent?* Earlier I mentioned the interconnectedness of all doctrines and the need for theology to attend to these relationships. Systematic consistency first involves orienting our doctrines correctly around the doctrine of God. "A systematic theology cannot be arranged simply as a string of topics. . . . The question of the relation of all these topics to the doctrine of God must determine the arrangement."[41] Secondarily, however, we must see whether holding to this particular proposal in, say, Christology puts any strain on other doctrines. Inconsistency can, as we saw, lead to heresy, but it more often leads to unfortunate imbalances and robs other doctrines of their vitality. Put differently, systematic inconsistency can cause varying degrees of damage to a theological system.

3. *Do its philosophical concepts control or clarify Scripture's teaching?* Barth once asked, "Why should theology not also employ current ideas, concepts, images, and expressions? As long as these prove themselves suitable, why could they not be 'eclectically' used with the greatest confidence?"[42] Philosophical concepts *are* often helpful in illuminating the Bible's teaching. However, sometimes they import baggage that distorts Christian teaching. At other times it can be wrongly assumed that the philosophical and biblical concepts are one and the same. For example, fourteenth-century Christian mystic Meister Eckhart borrowed from Plotinus when he wrote of believers "becoming one with the One." This language could imply that the Absolute One of Plotinus is the very same as the Christian God. Ultimately, Eckhart, a trinitarian, was unsuccessful in trying to reconcile the two conceptions of God. The resulting doctrine of God struggled to maintain the orthodox teaching on God as three persons, one essence.[43] Conversely, one could look at the concepts

---

41. Webster, *Domain of the Word*, 145.

42. Karl Barth, *Evangelical Theology: An Introduction*, trans. Grover Foley (Grand Rapids: Eerdmans, 1979), 91.

43. Clark, *To Know and Love God*, 306–7.

used in classical Christology as helpful in clarifying the reality of the
incarnate Word.

4. *Does its rationality conflict with Scripture's rationality?* Since
rationality is not merely something innate but also something learned
culturally, sometimes what seems plausible according to my rationality
may conflict with the Bible's rationality. Our cultural, learned rationality is what Lints calls "external reason," while Scripture's plausibility
structures are "internal reason." While we must assume significant
overlap between the two, they can be at odds. In this case, Scripture
sets the parameters for the conversation and provides the resources to
resolve the tension. Take, for example, the rationality of the doctrine
of the two natures of Christ. Some would see the divine attributes
as completely incompatible with human nature. Thus the biblical
doctrine of the incarnation of the Word would be contradictory. How
might this problem be resolved in a way that respects Scripture and
rationality, internal and external reason? First, we acknowledge the
Creator-creature distinction as foundational. Second, we assert the
Bible's primacy in setting the boundaries for the discussion. Third,
we examine what Scripture clearly affirms about Christ, such as his
actual birth, his full humanity, his preexistence as the Word, and so
forth. The believer must allow these teachings to set the agenda and
dictate what is plausible and what is not. So the question becomes
how these things can be so, rather than *that* they can be so. Finally,
we carefully use whatever concepts help clarify the doctrine of the
incarnation.[44]

Conclusion: To Believe Possible Things

Theology is not an escape from reason. It is an exercise of the created
and redeemed mind seeking to discern the rationality of God and the
world he created. This chapter sketches some of the issues involved
in the conversation between theology and reason and outlines things
to consider when assessing the rationality of one's theology. Theologians must seek to be coherent, consistent, and cogent, making

44. Richard Lints, *The Fabric of Theology: A Prolegomenon to Evangelical
Theology* (Eugene, OR: Wipf and Stock, 1999), 132–34.

every effort to speak the truth. Yet rationality is not independent of Scripture. John Paul II writes, "The results of reasoning may in fact be true, but these results acquire their true meaning only if they are set within the larger horizon of faith."[45] In theology, there is always a conversation consisting of unequal dialogue partners: Scripture has the louder voice but never shuts its ears to the voice of reason. As critical readers, we are called to sharpen our reasoning faculty so that we are not like the White Queen, believing "six impossible things before breakfast."

---

45. John Paul II, *Fides et Ratio*, http://w2.vatican.va/content/john-paul-ii/en/encyclicals/documents/hf_jp-ii_enc_14091998_fides-et-ratio.html.

6

The Trial of Real Life

Theology and Experience

There can be no doubt that all our knowledge begins with experience.

—Immanuel Kant, *Critique of Pure Reason*

In none of the twelve articles of faith can "I believe" be replaced by "I experience."

—Herman Bavinck, *Reformed Dogmatics*

In September 1954, a local midwestern newspaper ran the following headline: "Prophecy from Planet. Clarion Call to City: Flee That Flood. It'll Swamp Us on Dec. 21, Outer Space Tells Suburbanite." The description of the events is as follows:

Lake City will be destroyed by a flood from Great Lake just before dawn, Dec. 21, according to a suburban housewife. Mrs. Marian Keech, of 847 West School Street, says the prophecy is not her own. It is the purport of many messages she has received by automatic writing, she says. . . . The messages, according to Mrs. Keech, are sent to her by superior beings from a planet called "Clarion." These beings have been visiting the earth, she says, in what we call flying saucers. During their visits, she says, they have observed faultlines in the earth's crust that foretoken the deluge. Mrs. Keech reports she was told the flood will spread to form an inland sea stretching from the Arctic Circle to the Gulf of Mexico. At the same time, she says, a cataclysm will submerge the West Coast from Seattle, Wash., to Chile in South America.[1]

"Marian Keech" (whose real name is Dorothy Martin) began to channel messages from extraterrestrial beings (known to her as the Guardians) several months before the events recorded in the article above. She would receive messages about how the earth was dark and under the sway of Lucifer, but the forces of Light, beginning with Jesus, were trying to turn humanity away from its destructive paths. Her most notable message involved a catastrophic flood: the Great Lakes rising, buildings crumbling, a washing over of the earth, and the creation of a new order of humanity; France and England would be submerged in the Atlantic; Russia would become one great sea; Egypt would be remade, and the desert would become a fertile valley—and all these events would begin on December 21. Before the flood, however, she and her followers would be rescued by spaceship.

In the days leading up to doomsday, Keech and her followers gathered in her home in Lake City. They were told in messages that the flying saucers would pick them up on December 17 from Keech's backyard. When the rescue did not occur, they received further messages telling them that December 18 was the day, then midnight of the twenty-first. Still nothing. To add insult to injury, the flooding of the earth never occurred on the day foretold. With their hopes dashed, how did the believers respond? This is where things get interesting. Rather than accept the possibility that their beliefs were misguided or incorrect, they responded by (1) rationalizing why the flood and deliverance did not occur (e.g., the spacecraft would have frightened the people of earth; the Guardians delayed for wise but unknown reasons); (2) stretching the truth regarding their initial claims to avoid

1. Leon Festinger et al., *When Prophecy Fails* (London: Pinter & Martin, 2009), 32–33. My subsequent account of these events is taken chiefly from this volume.

admitting the falsity of their beliefs; (3) more actively proselytizing; and (4) offering more and more predictions in the hopes that one would come true. When presented with irrefutable evidence and when their experience (or lack thereof) disconfirmed their beliefs, they did not renounce these beliefs but held to them more tenaciously.

Psychologist Leon Festinger, who (along with two colleagues) studied this group extensively, has proposed a now-popular theory known as cognitive dissonance.[2] The theory describes the feeling of discomfort people experience when they have beliefs, opinions, actions, or knowledge that do not fit well together and the lengths they go to reduce or eliminate the dissonance or inconsistency. According to Festinger, people may acquire new information that will lessen the dissonance between the beliefs or experiences or minimize the importance of one of the dissonant beliefs as a way of rationalizing their belief or behavior and achieving less dissonance. The believers in our story coped with their cognitive dissonance in precisely those ways: they sought new predictions and messages from the Guardians, and they explained away and minimized the fact that the spaceship and the flood never came. Dissonance relieved. Beliefs remain intact.

● ● ● ● ●

Many of us would want to tell Keech and her followers that they need to face up to the facts. Their experience was telling the truth about their beliefs, but they were actively choosing to ignore it. This seems the height of folly, especially in an area as important as one's spiritual life. We intuitively know that our beliefs or opinions about the world need to correspond to the world itself. If experience contradicts a previously held opinion, then the opinion may need to be adjusted, if not rejected. This kind of thinking is true but not straightforward in the field of theology. Theologians throughout time, but especially in the last three hundred years, have stressed the need for consonance between our beliefs and our experience of God and God's world.[3]

2. See Leon Festinger, *A Theory of Cognitive Dissonance* (Stanford, CA: Stanford University Press, 1957).

3. It would have been appropriate to include much of the discussion of experience under the heading of reason. At the center of much controversy in the history of modern philosophy is the question of the sources used in thinking rationally. One

Calvin suggests as much when he writes about how we come to know God the Creator: "Indeed, with experience as our teacher we find God just as he declares himself in his Word."[4] John Wesley titled his treatise on original sin *The Doctrine of Original Sin, according to Scripture, Reason, and Experience.*[5] For him the biblical doctrine is manifest in and confirmed by experience, not only our experience of the Scriptures, but even our everyday observations and experience of the world. Experience matters to theology, as both teacher and judge, in its formulation and in our assessments of it. This chapter thus focuses on the place of experience in theology. We will begin by further exploring the difficulties and challenges of including experience among the other sources and criteria for theology. We will then outline various forms of experience and address how they might corroborate or correct one's theology. The chapter closes with principles to guide the careful use of experience as a tool for evaluating theology.

The Perils of Experience in Theology

Although "experience" has to some degree always been part of the church's development of theology, it usually comes last, if at all, in many modern discussions of theology's sources and criteria.[6] There are a number of reasons for this. First, experience is a notoriously broad and slippery notion. What counts as experience, and whose

---

camp, the empiricists, holds that all knowledge comes from (sense) experience of the world. Rationalists hold that our knowledge is not grounded in something extrinsic but rather something intrinsic, namely, our own minds. But it is obvious that when we are talking about reason's role in theology, we can also be talking about experience. While experience could have been included in the previous chapter, it is discussed here for the sake of thinking about experience more broadly than sense experience in the scientific and philosophical sense.

4. John Calvin, *Calvin: Institutes of the Christian Religion*, ed. John T. McNeill, trans. Ford Lewis Battles (Louisville: Westminster John Knox, 1960), I.10.2.

5. See Randy Maddox, ed., *The Works of John Wesley*, vol. 12, *Doctrinal and Controversial Treatises I* (Nashville: Abingdon, 2012), 155.

6. For example, the ancient saying "*lex orandi, lex credenda*"—that what is prayed indicates what should be believed—already points to the idea that the experience of worship shapes the formulation of doctrine. For a fuller discussion of this principle, see Geoffrey Wainwright, *Doxology: The Praise of God in Worship, Doctrine and Life: A Systematic Theology* (New York: Oxford University Press, 1984), chap. 7.

experience counts as a norm for theological reflection? Second, especially in modern liberal theology, experience has often supplanted Scripture, tradition, and reason as the norm for theological claims, thus fostering a reluctance on the part of many theologians to treat it at all.[7] Let us examine each of these issues.

The Ambiguity of Experience

When theologians use the word "experience," it is easy but unwise to assume that they are all talking about the same thing. As Rudolph Eucken said, "The term 'experience' has in the course of time become ever more ambiguous and in individual thinkers is subject to so many variations that it can hardly be considered a fixed term."[8] For the Reformers and their followers "experience" referred primarily to the living out of the truths of Scripture. Put differently, experience was religious and ethical in nature. Such experiences occur in all religions, including Christianity, and include the following: "A sense of guilt, pangs of conscience, doubt, unbelief, the feeling of God-forsakenness, longing for God, communion with God, delight in God, desire for and a sense of the forgiveness of sin, a thirst for holiness, and many more."[9] These experiences are part and parcel of the Christian life and accompany our assent to theological truths.

In the modern period, the notion of experience expanded to include findings generally attainable by observing the world—a kind of empiricism. Experience took on a scientific and philosophical character. In the early nineteenth century, the meaning further broadened to include what some camps describe as a particular kind of feeling shared by all humans—of "utter dependence" or "God-consciousness" or awareness of the transcendent or "God's gift of love."[10]

7. Ellen T. Charry, "Experience," in *The Oxford Handbook of Systematic Theology*, ed. John Webster, Kathryn Tanner, and Iain Torrance (Oxford: Oxford University Press, 2009), 413–18, 424.

8. Rudolph Eucken, quoted in Herman Bavinck, *Reformed Dogmatics*, vol. 1, *Prolegomena*, ed. John Bolt, trans. John Vriend (Grand Rapids: Baker Academic, 2003), 533.

9. Bavinck, *Reformed Dogmatics*, 1:533.

10. See, e.g., Friedrich Schleiermacher, *The Christian Faith*, ed. H. R. Mackintosh and J. S. Stewart (London: T&T Clark, 1999), 17, 47.

In the mid-twentieth century, experiences became more particularized and politically oriented. Black, feminist, and liberation theologies focused on the experience of particular oppressed groups: black people, women, and poor people living in the "third world."[11] To these could be added other experiences such as the communal experience of the church in worship. But the point is that when we ask how and if experience functions as a source or criterion for theology, we need to be clear about that to which we refer because an answer will often depend on the kind of experience about which we speak.

The Liberal Use of Experience

The greater concern of theologians regarding experience involves how it has overtaken Scripture, tradition, and reason as the primary authority in theology during the modern period. Schleiermacher is commonly viewed as the father of what many classify as the modern liberal approach to theology. George Lindbeck sums up the view well in four points:

1. Different religions are diverse expressions of a common core experience.
2. While the experience is a conscious one, it may be unknown on the level of self-conscious reflection (i.e., it is primal and not articulable).
3. The experience is present in all human beings.
4. The experience is the ultimate source and norm of the expressions of the experience. That is, the adequacy of religious expression is judged by the experience itself.[12]

Every religion is an expression of a common experience of the divine referred to as "the feeling of absolute dependence," "being grasped by ultimate concern," "being in love without restrictions," or "the experience of grace."[13] At the foundation of religion is not

11. Charry, "Experience," 414–16.
12. George A. Lindbeck, *The Nature of Doctrine: Religion and Theology in a Postliberal Age*, underlining ed. (Philadelphia: Westminster John Knox, 1984), 31.
13. Descriptions of the core experience provided (in order) by Friedrich Schleiermacher, Paul Tillich, Bernard Lonergan, and Karl Rahner.

something given in propositions or even narratives. Rather, the foundation is a conscious or preconscious experience of something ineffable, which in turn norms our speech about the experience. This is a deliberate move away from grounding theology in Scripture or tradition. How does this play out in doing and assessing theology? The following is an example of how one theologian (in this case, Schubert Ogden) applies this approach:[14]

1. A theological statement is appropriate if it is derived from or coherent with the specifically Christian experience of God in Christ as found in the earliest layer of the church's witness.
2. A theological statement is meaningful and true if it can be verified or justified by any of the following:
   a. The common or universal experience and reason of modern secular people
   b. The standards of experience and reason to which scientific thought is subject
   c. The universally human experience of the gift and demand of authentic experience
   d. Whether or not the church lives up to the demands implied by the theological statement

Another approach, taken by theologian Langdon Gilkey, follows a similar pattern:

1. A theological statement is meaningful only if it brings out a dimension of common secular experience and provides an answer to or resolution of an existential question.
2. A theological statement is valid only if it is able to interpret all areas of experience in an ontology (i.e., provides an ontological description of all areas of experience).
3. A theological statement is valid only if it mediates an experience of the divine presence and is thus verified in the experience and life of the religious community.

14. Both of the following summaries of Ogden and Gilkey are taken directly from Owen C. Thomas, "Theology and Experience," *Harvard Theological Review* 78, no. 1/2 (1985): 185, 188.

This approach can take on various permutations as we substitute one kind of experience (e.g., common secular experience) for another (e.g., the experience of the poor). Yet without concerning ourselves with the details of each account, it is simply worth noting that their starting point as well as their chief criterion for judging theological proposals is common (sometimes secular) human experience. This approach was and is appealing because it no longer needs to face the concerns raised by biblical criticism regarding the Bible's ability to provide sufficient warrant for theological proposals. Moreover, by focusing on the facts of religious or common human experience, theology can be viewed as scientific and regain its seat at the table in the academy. It can be seen as more respectable in the eyes of modern secular science.[15]

While these and other advantages have been attractive to scores of theologians, this view has come under serious attack. Lindbeck, for example, calls the idea of a common core experience "logically and empirically vacuous" since it is difficult, if not impossible, to identify the distinctive features of this experience shared by all religions.[16] In fact, the various religions interpret the primal experience in contradictory ways, thus exacerbating the difficulty of trying to understand the common core. The idea of a common experience is vague and unverifiable. Even if we abandon the notion of common experience and focus on the experiences of particular groups (as in liberation theologies), we are not much better off. Starting with the experience of the poor, for example, has brought with it the suspicion that Christianity is being used to further another sociopolitical agenda.[17] Put another way, this method wrongly locates Christian identity in the experience being advocated rather than in Christ, which is wrongheaded, not to mention arbitrary.[18]

Moreover, the appeal to *Christian* religious experience cannot account for more particular doctrines such as that Christ is God's only begotten Son or that God exists in three persons. Bavinck quips, "In

15. Bavinck, *Reformed Dogmatics*, 1:524.

16. Lindbeck, *Nature of Doctrine*, 32.

17. Jürgen Moltmann, *Experiences in Theology: Ways and Forms of Christian Theology* (Minneapolis: Fortress, 2000), 294–95.

18. Kevin J. Vanhoozer, *The Drama of Doctrine: A Canonical-Linguistic Approach to Christian Theology* (Louisville: Westminster John Knox, 2005), 19.

none of the twelve articles of faith can 'I believe' be replaced by 'I experience.'"[19] He observes the potential arbitrariness of theologies arising from Christian religious experience, noting, "One theologian infers from his experience a complete Lutheran dogmatics, another constructs from it only the reality of the person of Christ as Redeemer or as a moral example; a third, following this procedure, winds up having no Christianity left. Religious experience is such a subjective and individualistic principle that it opens the door to all sorts of arbitrariness in religion and actually enthrones anarchism: religion as a private thing."[20]

Vanhoozer comes to the same conclusion: "Christian experience on its own is too varied and unreliable to serve as the ultimate criterion for our knowledge of God."[21] If experience is fraught with such difficulties, is there any reason to retain it as a criterion for theology? If, as in Luther, the cross often contradicts experience, what do we make of the latter? Alister McGrath proposes that theology and experience may positively interact in three ways: theology (1) addresses experience, (2) interprets experience, and (3) transforms experience.[22] Is the only relationship between theology and experience, then, unidirectional, with theology addressing experience but not vice versa? If we, like McGrath and others, reject the liberal theological use of experience, can experience be salvaged? Given the ambiguity of the term, is it even worth salvaging? Difficulties notwithstanding, experience is something worth retaining as a criterion in theology, but only after we clearly identify what we are talking about. Once we are clear on that, we can move on to discuss its proper role in theology. These topics are the focus of the next section.

Whose Experience? Whose Theology? Experience as a Contribution

The term "experience," as we have seen, can be something of a wax nose. However, it does not defy definition. Drawing on definitions

---

19. Bavinck, *Reformed Dogmatics*, 1:534. Of course, this must be taken with a grain of salt in light of the fact that the experience of worship shaped Christian dogma from the earliest centuries.

20. Bavinck, *Reformed Dogmatics*, 1:535.

21. Vanhoozer, *Drama of Doctrine*, 6.

22. Alister McGrath, "Theology and Experience: Reflections on Cognitive and Experiential Approaches to Theology," *European Journal of Theology* 2, no. 1 (1993): 67–73.

offered by McGrath and Bavinck,[23] I would describe experience as encompassing knowledge arising from first- and secondhand personal and communal encounters with life, as well as perception and observation; it has to do with impressions, insights, and information we receive from outside ourselves, that is, from God and the created world. In describing experience this way, I am trying to include the religious and the nonreligious as well as the individual and the communal aspects of experience. I am also trying to account for the fact that experiences are not always firsthand but are often mediated to us through others. With this definition in mind, I want to probe how three forms of experience contribute to theology and become criteria for its validity: religious experience, experience of the world, and cultural experience.

Personal and Communal Religious Experience

"Confirming interpretation of Scripture by religious experiences . . . is the most comprehensive method of discovering genuine knowledge of a religious nature," notes theologian Don Thorsen.[24] The forcefulness of this claim may be off-putting to some, but most would agree to the related and more benign claim that our experience of God, whether in personal communion or communal worship, shapes our doctrine. While contributing to knowledge of God, experience does so ex post facto, primarily as confirmation of what was received from other sources such as Scripture. John Wesley, for example, reflected on the spiritual lives of "perfected" Christians as a way of fine-tuning and confirming his developing understanding of the doctrine of sanctification. In the middle of his *Plain Account of Christian Perfection*, he includes a lengthy account of the last days of one Jane Cooper, whom he describes as "a living and a dying witness of Christian perfection." After stating that "it [would] not be at all foreign to the subject" to include her story, Wesley quotes at length from a personal letter from Cooper who, after much anguish of soul and straining after holiness, writes:

---

23. McGrath, "Theology and Experience," 65; Bavinck, *Reformed Dogmatics*, 1:533.
24. Don Thorsen, *The Wesleyan Quadrilateral: Scripture, Tradition, Reason and Experience as a Model of Evangelical Theology* (Lexington: Emeth, 2005), 143.

I was in a moment enabled to lay hold on Jesus Christ, and found salvation by simple faith. He assured me, the Lord, the King was in the midst of me, and that I should see evil no more. I now blessed Him, who had visited and redeemed me, and was become my "wisdom, righteousness, sanctification, and redemption." I saw Jesus altogether lovely; and knew He was mine in all His offices. And glory be to Him, He now reigns in my heart without a rival. I find no will but His. I feel no pride; nor any affection but what is placed on Him. I know it is by faith I stand; and that watching unto prayer must be the guard of faith. I am happy in God at this moment, and I believe for the next.[25]

Here is concrete proof of the doctrine in the life of Jane Cooper. Wesley would go on to cite a certain "eye and ear witness" of Cooper's experience, one who stood by her at her death and could corroborate the truth of her experience.[26] This experience was not unique to Cooper but in fact was shared by many others. Wesley opens the next section of *Plain Account* by noting the reasons for further reflections on the doctrine: "The next year, *the number of those who believed they were saved from sin still increasing*, I judged it needful to publish."[27] The religious experience of growing numbers of people was proof positive of the doctrine and further impetus for writing about it. Not only did Wesley defend the reality of the doctrine by the lived experience of Christians; he also nuanced the doctrine through observed experience. When dealing with the question of whether one can fall from Christian perfection, he responds, "I am well assured they can: matter of fact puts this beyond dispute. Formerly we thought, one saved from sin could not fall; now we know the contrary. *We are surrounded with instances of those who lately experienced all that I mean by perfection.* They had both the fruit of the Spirit, and the witness; but they have now lost both." Concerning whether those who have fallen may recover the state of perfection, he answers tersely, "Why not? *We have many instances of this also.* Nay, it is an exceeding common thing for persons to lose it

25. John Wesley, *A Plain Account of Christian Perfection*, in *The Works of John Wesley*, vol. 13, *Doctrinal and Controversial Treatises II*, ed. Kenneth J. Collins and Paul Wesley Chilcote, bicentennial ed. (Nashville: Abingdon, 2013), 183–84.

26. Wesley, *Plain Account of Christian Perfection*, 184.

27. Wesley, *Plain Account of Christian Perfection*, 187 (emphasis added).

more than once, before they are established therein."[28] The religious
experience of "many" people demonstrates even the details of the
particular doctrine.

Along similar lines, British revivalist Smith Wigglesworth recounts
his rapturous experience of Spirit baptism with the accompanying
sign of tongues as evidence of the Pentecostal teaching. After having someone lay hands on him, the "fire fell." He goes on: "Then
He gave me a revelation. Oh, it was wonderful! He showed me an
empty cross and Jesus glorified. . . . Then I saw that God had puri-
fied me. I was conscious of the cleaning of the precious blood of
Jesus, and I cried out, 'Clean! Clean! Clean!' . . . As I was extolling,
glorifying, and praising Him, I was speaking in tongues 'as the Spirit
gave [me] utterance'" (Acts 2:4). He concludes confidently: "What
had I received? I had received the Bible evidence. This Bible evidence
is wonderful to me. I knew I had received the very evidence of the
Spirit's incoming that the Apostles received on the day of Pentecost.
I knew that everything I had had up to that time was in the nature of
an anointing bringing me in line with God in preparation, but now
I knew I had the Biblical Baptism in the Spirit."[29]

The doctrine is evidenced by experience. The two go hand in
hand. Of course this does preclude the possibility that our experiences may prove false or fabricated or that our interpretation of those
experiences may be incorrect, as some might say of the doctrines
presented in the two prior examples. Yet we can still observe that
the methodological moves are not all that strange. Worship or our
experience of God is, as McGrath puts it, "the crucible within which
theological statements are refined."[30] And as with all refinement, there
is a burning away (of falsehoods) and a verification or purification
(bringing out the truth more manifestly).

In his instructions to young theologians, Helmut Thielicke admon-
ishes his hearers to pay close attention to what he calls "the spiritual

28. John Wesley, *Farther Thoughts on Christian Perfection*, in *Works of John Wesley*, 13:110 (emphasis added).
29. Smith Wigglesworth, *Smith Wigglesworth on the Holy Spirit* (New Kensington, PA: Whitaker House, 1999), 49–50.
30. Alister E. McGrath, *The Genesis of Doctrine: A Study in the Foundation of Doctrinal Criticism* (Grand Rapids: Eerdmans, 1997), 58.

instinct of the children of God." By this he means the spiritual wisdom that ordinary Christians have gained through the experience of walking with Christ. This experience, though uninformed at times, is not to be ignored because it can give pause to our theology. The church, in its experiences of God, is the theologian's pastor.[31] Schleiermacher offers his own version when he claims that doctrinal propositions must be presented in such a way "that *every fellow believer* may verify them at once by the certainty of his own immediate religious self-consciousness."[32] Doctrines are confirmed by the collective religious experience of the church.

All this is simply a fancy way of saying that the lived experience of the Christian life provides knowledge and insight into the truths of Scripture and is thus an indispensable resource for doing theology. In fact, our doctrine is fine-tuned and nuanced in the crucible of an actual Christian life. By way of an example, a soldier can learn all about war in military academy and simulated training exercises, but he learns with depth the nature of war when he is on the battlefield. It is then that he will be able to articulate with greater intricacy what war is and is not about and how one should engage. Similarly, less experienced Christians, generally speaking, will lack the kind of insight into certain doctrines (i.e., teachings of Scripture) that more mature believers possess.[33] Indeed, Scripture reminds us to "taste and see that the LORD is good," that is, to know by trial and experience the divine attribute of goodness (Ps. 34:8). All things being equal, those who have tasted are likely better positioned to test accounts of divine goodness than those who have not.

What all this suggests is that doctrine must undergo the trial of real life. Theology cannot sidestep the test of our experience and is, in fact, enriched by careful attention to the religious lives of individuals and church communities. When we encounter a theological proposal

31. Helmut Thielicke, *A Little Exercise for Young Theologians*, trans. Charles L. Taylor (Grand Rapids: Eerdmans, 2003), 26.

32. Admittedly, it seems he is dealing more with dogma than with an individual's theology or smaller points of teaching. Friedrich Schleiermacher, *Brief Outline on the Study of Theology*, trans. Terrence N. Tice (Richmond: John Knox, 1966), 76 (emphasis added).

33. See John M. Frame, *The Doctrine of the Knowledge of God* (Phillipsburg, NJ: P&R, 1987), 334–35.

(one that can be tested by experience), we must ask if it is expressive
of and true to the Christian's experience of God.

Experience of the World: Science and the Day-to-Day

Beyond religious experience, another form of experience imposes
itself on theology, namely, what one might call general human experience of the world. What I have in mind are the observations we make
of the world God has made, which may arise with little conscious
effort from the layperson or with the methodological rigor of the
scientist. Whatever the path, the question that occupies us is how
experience understood in this way might inform theology as well
as function as a criterion for its assessment. Famed agnostic T. H.
Huxley saw the relationship between science and theology as fairly
straightforward. He once wrote, "Extinguished theologians lie about
the cradle of every science as the strangled snakes beside that of
Hercules; and history records that whenever science and orthodoxy
have been fairly opposed, the latter has been forced to retire from the
lists, bleeding and crushed if not annihilated; scotched, if not slain.
But orthodoxy is the Bourbon of the world of thought. It learns not,
neither can it forget."[34]

According to Huxley, scientific observation has often snuffed out
dogma because the latter is unwilling to think and is often founded
on little more than opinion. To those who hold such a view, theology
should concede that it is the lesser partner in the conversation between
the two disciplines. In fact, the dialogue is more like a monologue: if
the two partners conflict, science trumps theology—period. Is there
some truth to this conception of the relationship between the two?

One scholar of religion and science cautions that we begin discussions of their relationship by acknowledging that this interaction is manifold and complicated, rich and fascinating, rather than
monolithic or black and white.[35] This warning coincides with the
tendency some have to ignore the particular ways that particular

34. Thomas Henry Huxley, *Darwiniana: Essays*, vol. 2 of *Collected Essays* (New
York: D. Appleton, 1912), 52.
35. See John Hedley Brooke, *Science and Religion: Some Historical Perspectives*
(Cambridge: Cambridge University Press, 1991).

sciences interact with particular strands of theology. In essence, we are not asking how "science" relates to "theology" but how specific findings in, say, geology or biology, relate to specific theological commitments concerning creation or anthropology.[36] With that cautionary word in mind, we may still sketch some positive ways the two disciplines have related. First, science *may* be a stimulus for theology, thus allowing theologians to analyze whether they have correctly interpreted Scripture or even whether they have fallen prey to other (maybe outdated) scientific theories in their articulation of Christian doctrine.[37] For example, evolutionary theories have, at the very least, caused theologians to revisit Scripture and its teachings on the earth's origins. Second, scientific conclusions *may* confirm certain theological claims. For example, the study of genetics has been used to argue for the existence of an intelligent designer.

But the question that interests most people is, Can science trump theology? By this, one is usually asking whether science has an authority comparable to or greater than Scripture. This question is answered in two ways. First, straightforwardly: we must allow that a scientific insight *can* disconfirm a theological belief. If a community of theologians deems a specific scientific insight well founded, they may find the need to tweak or reject prior theological understandings. The classic example of this is how Copernican astronomy—the heliocentric solar system—displaced the Ptolemaic view that held sway for two thousand years. Second, the question must be answered with some clarity and nuance. If perchance a scientific idea did lead to the altering of a theological belief, this would not necessarily amount to a rejection of Scripture or its authority. If we describe theology as most fundamentally the *interpretation* of Scripture, then science—the interpretation of the cosmos—is merely calling into question an interpretation rather than the Bible itself. For example, Christian proponents of an old earth appeal to astronomical and geological evidence in order to question the biblical interpretation—or theology—of young earth advocates while maintaining the authority of the Bible.

36. David K. Clark, *To Know and Love God: Method for Theology*, Foundations of Evangelical Theology (Wheaton: Crossway, 2003), 284.

37. Alister E. McGrath, *A Scientific Theology*, vol. 1, *Nature* (Grand Rapids: Eerdmans, 2001), 60–64.

David Clark summarizes the issue: "The better way to think of this is to say that for evangelical theology, both theology (interpretations of special revelation) and science (interpretations of general revelation) come under the authority of Scripture itself."[38] In some cases, the best response to tensions between theology and science is patience—allowing time for our grasp of theology or of science to adjust and so relieve the tension. In the end, if theology is concerned with the question of truth, it must reckon with truth mediated through the ordered observation and experience of the world.

We may extend these claims to the more commonplace human experiences. If we describe perception as a form of everyday experience, then it certainly has a place in theological reflection and assessment. Jesus often anchors his teaching in common human perceptions or observations of such things as the birds of the air and the flowers of the field (Matt. 6:26–34), how people use lamps (Matt. 5:16), and what happens when people eat (Matt. 15:11). More importantly, to a large degree the Christian faith is rooted in perception: "That which was from the beginning, which we have *heard*, which we have *seen* with our eyes, which we have *looked at* and our hands have *touched*—this we proclaim concerning the Word of life" (1 John 1:1).[39] Collective perceptions of reality are an invaluable, even if not infallible, check on theological claims. A classic example is the appeal to the universal and pervasive reality of human sin, even among young children, as an argument for inherited sin. If experience shows that people sin at every time in history, among every culture, and at every age, then this strengthens the case for original sin.

At the same time, we must grant that our own interpretation and valuation of our experience may be wrong. We must also acknowledge that certain doctrines will be exempt from the test of experience. Nevertheless, we must allow that our eyes, ears, hands, and mind make sense of their input and give us access to reality rather than obscure it. Therefore, appeals to experience may strengthen a proposal rather than undermine it.

38. Clark, *To Know and Love God*, 285–86. See also his discussion of how theology speaks to the sciences (287–93).
39. Frame, *Doctrine of the Knowledge of God*, 334.

Total Human Experience: Culture

Closely related to the above discussion is the issue of culture. Culture, according to Lesslie Newbigin, is "the sum total of ways of living developed by a group of human beings and handed on from generation to generation."[40] Another writer describes it as "the sum of [a group's] learned behavior patterns, attitudes, and material things."[41] It is the "web of the total human experience in the world."[42] Culture includes the language, art, technology, social and political configurations, and religion (and theology) of a group. Culture is the collective experience of the past brought into and experienced in the present. In recent Western history, being "cultured" meant that someone had read the important works of the Western canon and had been exposed to the important works of Western art and music—what has been called a "classicist" notion of culture. Most have abandoned such a view in favor of an "empiricist" perspective that recognizes the existence of countless legitimate cultures with different values, a different "canon," and different art and music.[43] So if culture is the web of total experience of a *particular* group, how should it bear on theology and does it provide help in judging it?

The attempt to extricate culture from our theology is a futile one. As we saw in chapter 2, culture invariably shapes our theology by the mere fact that it is the context from which we do our theologizing. The way many tend to conceive of the relationship between culture and theology is to see culture as influencing a theologian unconsciously or indirectly, while a theologian's job is to speak back to culture directly, idiomatically, and prophetically. Although this is indeed part of the story, we can say something more about the positive role of culture in doing and assessing theology.

40. Lesslie Newbigin, *Foolishness to the Greeks: The Gospel and Western Culture* (Grand Rapids: Eerdmans, 1986), 3.

41. Edward T. Hall, *The Silent Language*, quoted in Clark, *To Know and Love God*, 100.

42. Richard Lints, *The Fabric of Theology: A Prolegomenon to Evangelical Theology* (Eugene, OR: Wipf and Stock, 1999), 104.

43. Stephen B. Bevans, *Models of Contextual Theology* (Maryknoll, NY: Orbis, 2002), 11. He is here borrowing from Bernard Lonergan, *Method in Theology*, vol. 1 (New York: Herder & Herder, 1972).

Culture contributes to the construction of theology in at least two positive ways. First, it poses particular important questions that theology must answer and prescribes a form theology must take if it is to be faithful to its evangelical calling to translate the gospel to every tribe and tongue. Black liberation theologian James Cone raises this issue, writing, "One's social and historical context decides not only the questions we address to God but also the mode or form of the answers given to the questions."[44] Liberationist theologies like Cone's are an obvious example of this claim regarding culture's contribution, and it may be worth reflecting for a moment on the value of the approach for theology more broadly.

Cone asserts that the faithful theologian is one who asks the right questions and looks to the right sources for answers. What are the right questions? He writes, "The right questions are always related to the basic question: What has the gospel to do with the oppressed of the land and their struggle for liberation? Any theologian who fails to place that question at the center of his or her work has ignored the essence of the gospel."[45] This driving question arises from the cultural experience of blacks in America, which is characterized by oppression. It is these questions, as well as those arising from other cultures' experiences, that drive theologians back to Scripture to look for particular answers to their own set of issues.

What can result is the unearthing of themes embedded in Scripture that are ignored because the usual questions asked by those cut off from the experience of the oppressed cannot elicit the right answers. This is what Cone bemoans about seminaries in America: "Unfortunately not only white seminary professors but some blacks as well have convinced themselves that only the white experience provides the appropriate context for questions and answers concerning things divine. They do not recognize the narrowness of their experience and the particularity of their theological expressions. They like to think of themselves as *universal* people. . . . They fail to recognize that other people also have thought about God and have something significant to say about Jesus' presence in the world."[46]

44. James H. Cone, *God of the Oppressed*, rev. ed. (Maryknoll, NY: Orbis, 1997), 14.
45. Cone, *God of the Oppressed*, 9.
46. Cone, *God of the Oppressed*, 14.

The notion that Cone advances is not necessarily to deny the legitimacy of questions arising from a majority white, Western culture. Rather, it is to legitimize the questions arising from other voices and to see them as valuable for theology. Is not God's care for the marginalized a significant theme in the Old Testament? Does not the theme of oppression—spiritual and otherwise—emerge in Jesus's proclamation of his mission? One does not need to agree with the answers Cone or other liberationists provide to see that they are asking valuable questions about the gospel and kingdom that often go unasked, to the detriment of the theology of the church universal. Speaking of less "radical" theologians like Augustine, Luther, Wesley, and Barth, Hendrikus Berkhof sums up the matter well. "Some theologians have a special gift for sensing the shifts taking place in a given culture and in the human mind; they are people who experience existence very differently from previous generations, and from their new vantage point they put new questions to the Bible and tradition, questions to which they clearly receive surprising new answers."[47] The point for our purposes is that the questions raised by culture can generate fruitful and creative (in the best sense) theological responses.

Closely related to this concern is a second contribution that culture makes to theology: it provides valuable insights into Scripture. Theologian Stephen Pardue observes, for instance, that the Nicene Creed and the Formula of Chalcedon would not have been possible apart from the tools provided by the Greek language and intellectual culture of the time. Concepts like *homoousios*, *hypostasis*, and *ousia*—local cultural ways of understanding being and personhood—have enabled future generations to reflect well on the Trinity and the person of Christ. He concludes, "In this very real sense, the church gained theological insights that would otherwise not have been available."[48]

These gains from culture are not just a phenomenon of the early centuries of the church but rather are something we see today. One

47. Hendrikus Berkhof, *Introduction to the Study of Dogmatics* (Grand Rapids: Eerdmans, 1985), 24–25.

48. Stephen Pardue, "What Hath Wheaton to Do with Nairobi?," *Journal of the Evangelical Theological Society* 58, no. 4 (2015): 764–65. See also Lewis Ayres, *Nicaea and Its Legacy: An Approach to Fourth-Century Trinitarian Theology* (Oxford: Oxford University Press, 2006).

example can be drawn from what is known as the honor and shame culture of the Chinese and how it affects theologies of atonement and justification. Honor in these discussions refers to one's own sense of worth and the recognition by one's social group of that worth.[49] Shame involves a negative social evaluation of oneself; it focuses on the inadequacy or falling short of the self. "Shame is the disgrace which a sinner brings upon oneself and those associated with him."[50] Honor and shame have communal and covenantal overtones. When these concepts are translated into atonement theology, we can say that the work of Christ was to restore God's honor and remove our shame by Christ supremely honoring God and paying the honor debt, bearing the shame we rightly bear, so that we might receive the honor of being children of God. The chief focus of the atonement, then, is on God's honor and less so on God's law (though they are of course intertwined). The atonement is about repairing the familial and covenantal dishonor and shame caused by humanity's sins. It is about saving God's "face," which is a Chinese way of speaking about honor and shame.[51] My point here is that a cultural way of life contributes insight and enriches specific doctrines. And we should expect this to be the case if we believe in the church's catholicity. A classic example within Scripture is the *logos* theology of John 1, which likely draws from its Greco-Roman cultural context, and in doing so enriches our understanding of Christ. Indeed, every theology, birthed and nurtured in its local culture, has the potential to speak to other local theologies for the benefit of enhancing the church's total understanding of the gospel.

Experience—religious, general, or cultural—is an important contributor to doctrine. It is not the final arbiter of truth, but it does help us access such truth, as it both corroborates the teachings of Scripture and provides resources for better understanding it.

49. Bruce J. Malina, *The New Testament World: Insights from Cultural Anthropology* (Louisville: Westminster John Knox, 2001), 30. See also Jackson Wu, *Saving God's Face: A Chinese Contextualization of Salvation through Honor and Shame* (Pasadena, CA: William Carey International University Press, 2013), 148–92.

50. S. J. DeVries, "Shame," in *The Interpreter's Bible Dictionary*, vol. 4, ed. George A. Buttrick (New York: Abingdon, 1962), quoted in Wu, *Saving God's Face*, 149.

51. See Wu, *Saving God's Face*, chaps. 4 and 5.

The Salutarity of Theology: Experience as a Consequence

Experience is not only a contributor of content to theology; it is also a consequence of theology. What I have in mind is that theology, if it is done well, should lead to an experience of the good, true, and beautiful. Remember the conviction of Augustine, cited in chapter 1: "So anyone who thinks that he has understood the divine scriptures or any part of them, but cannot by his understanding build up this double love of God and neighbour, has not yet succeeded in understanding them."[52] Christian doctrine must produce virtue. Ellen Charry claims this to be the view adopted by most prominent premodern theologians:

> The theologians who shaped the tradition believed that God was work-ing with us to teach us something, to get our attention through the Christian story, including those elements of the story that make the least sense to us. They were interested in forming us as excellent persons. Christian doctrines aim to be good for us by forming or reforming our character. . . . The great theologians of the past . . . were striv-ing not only to articulate the meaning of the doctrines but also their pastoral value or salutarity—how they are good for us. . . . For these theologians, beauty, truth, and goodness—the foundation of human happiness—come from knowing and loving God and nowhere else.[53]

Theology seeks to discern the good toward which God, our divine teacher and parent, is directing us. Put another way, biblical doctrine is for our good; it is for our formation through the knowledge and experience of God. Charry's point is that when the great theologians theologized, they were not merely seeking to give a clear articulation of biblical teaching as an end in itself. Rather, they understood that even the most difficult and complex teachings of Scripture were meant for our good; that is, they aimed to be "salutary." Thus theological precision and pastoral aim were wedded together without any sense of impropriety. Two examples—a brief one from Athanasius and a lengthy one from Calvin—may suffice to illustrate this point.

52. Augustine, *On Christian Teaching*, trans. and ed. R. P. H. Green (Oxford: Oxford University Press, 2008), 27.
53. Ellen T. Charry, *By the Renewing of Your Minds: The Pastoral Function of Christian Doctrine* (New York: Oxford University Press, 1999), vii.

Athanasius and the Doctrine of Christ

Charry contends that Athanasius's treatment of the eternal relation between the Father and the Son had the pastoral aim of fostering
the good life among God's creatures. For Athanasius, the good life
resulted from abandoning the lesser gods of paganism and coming
to know God the Father properly. But since our knowledge of the
Father comes only through the Son, we must be able to articulate
with some precision their relationship as well as the Son's own nature,
to avoid understandings of God that lead to a less excellent life.[54] In
Contra Gentes, Athanasius is at pains to highlight the Son's eternal
relationship to the Father, one that is inherent and natural and not
by grace. He writes:

> Everything was created through him and for him, and that being good
> offspring of a good Father and true Son, he is the power of the Father
> and his wisdom and Word; not so by participation [*metochen*], nor
> do these properties accrue to him from outside in the way of those
> who participate [*metechontas*] in him are given wisdom by him, hav-
> ing their power and reason in him; but he is absolute light, absolute
> truth, absolute justice, absolute virtue, and indeed stamp, effulgence,
> and image. In short, he is the supremely perfect issue of the Father,
> and is alone Son, the express image of the Father.[55]

His concern in delineating the divine attributes of the Son is to
differentiate the Son's sonship from our own. But that is only the
beginning of the pastoral concern. If Christ became a son by grace
as we do and was not a son by nature, he could not reveal God to
us. This is a problem because according to John 17:3, the essence
of eternal life is knowing "the only true God, and Jesus Christ."
Whereas paganism led to debauchery and the deformation of the
soul, the knowledge of God leads to life and the restoration of the
divine image. When Athanasius would finally employ the technical
language of *homoousios*, his end was to show that Jesus Christ as

---

54. Charry, *By the Renewing of Your Minds*, 228–29.
55. Athanasius, *Contra Gentes*, 46:131, quoted in Ellen T. Charry, "The Case
for Concern: Athanasian Christology in Pastoral Perspective," *Modern Theology*
9, no. 3 (1993): 273.

God truly reveals the true God to us.[56] And in revealing God, Jesus provides the way to the good life, through the contemplation of God and the formation of virtue.

Calvin and the Doctrine of Election

In the *Institutes* of 1536, Calvin addresses the doctrine of election within his exposition of the nature of the church from the Apostles' Creed. The holy catholic church is the "whole number of the elect, whether angels or men," those gathered by God to be "one church and society, and one people of God."[57] The church is *holy* since all those whom God has chosen by his "eternal providence" he also objectively sanctifies in Christ; it is *catholic* because all God's elect are united in Christ, sharing one faith, hope, love, Spirit, and calling to eternal life.[58] Thus Calvin joins election in Christ with the sanctification and common life of the Christian community, election preceding and resulting in both.[59]

A central theme in Calvin's treatment of election, indeed the primary *function* of the doctrine of election, is that of assurance, and this is construed in three ways. First, objective assurance of salvation is rooted in eternal election. The immutability and invincibility of God's eternal purposes, coupled with the safekeeping of Christ vouchsafed to believers, guarantee the salvation of the elect.[60] Second, the subjective assurance of our election is found in our own faith in Christ—that is, those who presently trust in Christ are indeed those whom God has chosen from eternity.[61] Finally, Calvin cautions about the impossibility

---

56. Charry, "Case for Concern," 275.

57. John Calvin, *Institutes of the Christian Religion*, 1536 ed., trans. Ford Lewis Battles (Grand Rapids: Eerdmans, 1986), §21, 58.

58. Calvin, *Institutes* (1536), §21, 58.

59. Calvin is later able to speak of election as God's sanctifying for himself a people from the polluted mass of humanity (see §23, 59). He connects objective holiness to God's election, citing the latter as the grounds of the former. Those whom God has chosen are objectively (that is, by God) brought into the sphere of holiness and consecrated to serve God. Thus two themes that help to form the theological context for "reading" are wedded in Calvin's early treatment of election. In the 1559 edition of the *Institutes*, he makes election the ground of progressive sanctification (as we will see).

60. Calvin, *Institutes* (1536), §21, 59.

61. Calvin, *Institutes* (1536), §24, 60.

of decisively discerning another person's election. Although God has given us some marks by which we may discern those who belong to the people of God, only God knows absolutely who belongs to him. Therefore, if one professes faith in Christ and participates in the sacraments, he or she must be judged charitably as elect and a member of the church.[62] Thus the doctrine of election is meant to foster faith, patience, love of God, and charity toward neighbor.

Calvin's treatment of election in the *Institutes* of 1559 carries on his interest with eternal predestination. Although it is a difficult teaching, it is a profoundly useful one. Calvin notes, "We shall never be clearly persuaded, as we ought to be, that our salvation flows from the wellspring of God's free mercy until we come to know his eternal election, which illumines God's grace by this contrast: that he does not indiscriminately adopt all into the hope of salvation but gives to some what he denies to others."[63] The doctrine of election, therefore, is exceedingly useful because it exhibits the nature of salvation by drawing attention to the utter freedom and gratuitousness of God's favor. This hard teaching produces at least three salutary results for believers: (1) it humbles us because we contribute nothing to our redemption; (2) it causes us to feel how much we owe to God; and (3) it frees us from fear and assures us of God's continued care. Therefore, it is more detrimental to others to avoid teaching election than the opposite.[64] In fact, basing his argument on Ephesians 1:4–5, Calvin emphasizes the point that election precedes and empowers holiness, not vice versa.[65] Whatever good that comes from a believer's life is the fruit of his or her election. Thus election sets the context for understanding one's calling and vocation. In fact, when Calvin deals with the objection that his doctrine of eternal election destroys zeal for an upright life, he responds, "What a great difference there is between these two things: to cease well-doing because election is sufficient for salvation, and to devote ourselves to the pursuit of good

62. Calvin, *Institutes* (1536), §26, 61.
63. John Calvin, *Calvin: Institutes of the Christian Religion*, ed. John T. McNeill, trans. Ford Lewis Battles (Louisville: Westminster John Knox, 1960), III.21.1. Following citations refer to the 1960 edition.
64. Calvin, *Calvin: Institutes*, III.21.1, 921–2.
65. Calvin, *Calvin: Institutes*, III.22.2, 934.

as the appointed goal of election! Away, then, with such sacrileges, for they wickedly invert the whole order of election."[66] Rather than short-circuiting obedience and holiness, election, having the "pursuit of good" (however specified) as its "appointed goal," should fuel well-doing. We can see that even a doctrine so controversial, difficult to grasp, and unsavory (to some) is still angled toward the formation of virtue, ultimately for the sake of the good life in God.

Calvin's mention of well-doing points us to something that needs to be brought out more explicitly, namely, that good doctrine leads to good *public* practice. The virtue produced by good theology is not merely something inward with no outward dimension. Rather, virtue is others oriented; it directs itself to God and fellow humans. Good theology should produce practices that reflect the beauty, goodness, and truth of the kingdom of God. Barth writes, "For who can possibly see what is meant by the knowledge of God, His divine being, His divine perfections, the election of His grace, without an awareness at every point of the demand which is put to man by the fact that this God is his God, the God of man? . . . The dogmatics of the Christian Church, and basically the Christian doctrine of God, is ethics."[67] While the knowledge of false gods deforms the soul and leads to countless practices that debase humanity, the proper knowledge of the true God and his ways is what Charry calls "aretegenic" (virtue producing or conducive to virtue).[68] Theology and ethical consequence go hand in hand, and the latter may be carefully employed as a criterion for evaluating the relative success or failure of a doctrine.

Theology and Experience: Reflections and Principles

Throughout this chapter, I have tried to sketch some of the ways in which theology has been brought into conversation with various forms of experience. As I have done so, I hope that some principles (and

---

66. Calvin, *Calvin: Institutes*, III.23.12, 960–61.

67. Barth's chief point is that the doctrine of God is intrinsically ethical because to know God is to understand that he is Lord, the one who commands obedience and creates the freedom for it. However, the connection between knowing God and its proper results is helpful for our present point. See Barth, *CD* II/2, 512, 515.

68. Charry, *By the Renewing of Your Minds*, 19.

issues), at least in embryonic form, have taken root in the reader's mind. Let us draw out some of those guiding principles.

1. *Experience is not the starting point for theology* in principle, *though it may certainly be so as a matter of fact.* Theology is primarily reflection on the Word of God, and this must be the case since experience can be deceptive. Experience must always be reformed by the Word and sound theology. What this means, for example, is that we cannot assume that the questions asked of Scripture or theology by culture are the right questions. Even the questions posed must come under the judgment of the Word of God.

2. *Some doctrines are (likely) immune to the test of experience, and some will in fact contradict our experience.* For example, it is difficult to see how a doctrine of the Trinity or even eschatology is much advanced by experience or how they can be judged by human experience in any meaningful way. However, the doctrines of creation, sin, sanctification, anthropology, and ecclesiology might be sharpened and evaluated with the help of our experiences of God and the world. For instance, the study of psychology can show empirically how sin operates in the soul; it can show the precise shape of our pathologies and may inform how we speak about sin and how we heal from it.

3. With these qualifications in place, *we should ask if a theology is confirmed by our personal, and especially the church's, experience of the Christian life.* I emphasize the need for the collective experience of redeemed humanity to play the chief role, not the sole experience of the Christian or the experience of those unredeemed. The experience of those renewed by the Spirit is a check, even if not infallible, on the pronouncements of theologians. In addition, the credible results of "unredeemed" science or the regular experiences of the average person should cautiously be brought into conversation with theology. The insights of biology, psychology, geology, and day-to-day life can in principle trump theology, even if they may never be allowed to contradict Scripture. Our responsibility in such cases would be to find ways these can be reconciled with our ultimate authority, Scripture.

4. *Culture—as a form of experience—has some role to play in validating or invalidating theologies.* Concerns regarding parochialism

and subjectivism notwithstanding, we must evaluate theologies "culturally" in at least two ways.

a. *We have to ask about the theology's "fit" within a particular culture.* Does it speak to those particular concerns adequately? Does it speak with a language and concepts that are understandable? Does it speak of reality in a way that contradicts the reality of those who occupy this cultural space?

b. *To some extent all local or particular theologies must be able to be translated cross-culturally and address universal concerns.* Along these lines, we must ask whether such a translation fits with, precludes, or enhances other accounts of a doctrine. The universality (and, therefore, validity) of all local proposals is tied to whether it can sit at peace with other local proposals.

5. *Good theology forms good people.* Put differently, good theology leads to good practices. While this claim must be qualified in light of the fact that even doctrines like justification can appear to provide permission to sin that grace may abound, we may still see good fruit as *one* factor that contributes to the plausibility of a doctrine. The ultimate norm, again, is Scripture, for as a donkey can rebuke a "prophet," so rubbish can edify some by the mercy of God. One of the more vexing challenges for readers of theology is trying to discern whether bad fruit is the logical outcome of someone's theology or the result of deviating from said theology.[69] Nevertheless, we hold that false gods deform the soul, and untruth sets no one free to love God and neighbor. Doctrine and the life produced must be held together, even if the task of evaluating doctrine on the basis of its practical outcomes is a difficult one.

Conclusion: Jumping Our Own Shadow?

Responding to the question of whether theologians should try as hard as possible to exclude life experience from their theologizing,

---

69. Fred Sanders makes this point about Wesley's teaching on Christian perfection. See Fred Sanders, *Wesley on the Christian Life: The Heart Renewed in Love* (Wheaton: Crossway, 2013), 214–15.

Hendrikus Berkhof retorts, "But who can jump his own shadow?"[70] He is speaking of the inevitability of experience's influence on theology. We simply cannot escape it. But what I have advocated in this chapter is a more positive orientation to the role of experience in theological formulation and assessment. Experience is a trickier criterion for evaluating theologies than the others covered in this book, as one might have noticed from all the cautionary notes sprinkled throughout the chapter. Experience does not have the authority of Scripture or tradition and can be the cause of many theological missteps. Nevertheless, it is a criterion with which we must reckon, for it provides another way of confirming and refuting held beliefs. Whether as a contribution to or as a consequence of theology, experience confronts us, calling us to account for our doctrine and sometimes demanding that we face up to the inconvenient facts of real life.

70. Berkhof, *Introduction to the Study of Dogmatics*, 26.

Epilogue

Practice Makes Perceptive

I recently borrowed a friend's bike, having not ridden one for years. At first I was shaky, but as the saying goes: It's just like riding a bike. This ability to instinctively do something your body has not done in years is called "muscle memory"; you remember a skill because it has been hardwired into your brain. Hours and hours of a repeated task make performing the task instinctive. One of the most difficult lessons for my children to learn is that it takes time and practice to become excellent at most things. Whether learning to dribble a basketball or to play the piano, they often assume that mastery should come instantaneously. The prospect of having to dribble the ball one or two hundred times during practice, for example, is frustrating, and they feel defeated before they begin. What they need to understand is that something that at first requires a great deal of effort and concentration will eventually be done intuitively with little effort—if they are patient. What is true for most skills is also true for reading theology well: it takes time, effort, and perseverance.

This book is a primer for those wishing to sharpen their skills as readers of theology. Part 1 prepared readers to engage with theological literature more charitably by identifying issues that prevent us from reading others' theology with love. It sought to foster charity by calling readers to examine the antilove postures we adopt, as well as by directing readers to refrain from firm judgments of a doctrine until the author's backstory is known. Overcoming our internal obstacles to love does not mean that we cease to evaluate. Rather, it helps us do so from a posture that reflects Christ and facilitates learning.

In part 2, we began to identify and develop the critical skills necessary for reading theology. We examined the various ways theologians engage with Scripture, tradition, reason, and experience. Behind every theological proposal are myriad assumptions about the nature and role of these four sources. Our awareness of this variety is a vital stage in our development as theologians. Part 2 provided guiding principles for evaluating theologies with respect to each of these sources.

Now it is quite possible to come to the end of this book and feel overwhelmed by all this variety and the abundance of guiding principles that must be kept in view. But the easiest way to combat feeling overwhelmed is simple: *start small* and *start somewhere*.

First, choose a text (if one is not already assigned to you). Try beginning with any of the following:

- Theological classics
- A chapter from a theology textbook
- A journal article in contemporary theology
- A short reading from a text with which you are inclined to disagree

Once you have chosen a reading, do your best to discern the backstory. Here are some suggestions for discovering the context of a theologian or a theology:

- Read the preface, introduction, afterword, and epilogue of works written by the theologian. These often offer clues into the motives and circumstances surrounding the writing of the work.
- Look for clues *in* the text that signal the precipitating reason(s) of the writing (e.g., specific names, places, people, events mentioned).
- Find survey articles about the theologian's life (in dictionaries, encyclopedias, textbooks, handbooks, etc.) in order to understand their ecclesial and other contextual influences.

- Pay attention to repeated key words and ideas. These can be clues to the context—especially the churchly context.

Once you have filled in some of the details of the theology's context, move on to evaluate it on the basis of its engagement with Scripture. Try to become familiar with one or two of the guiding principles and attempt to apply them as best you can. For example, you may begin by asking, What aspect of Scripture is authoritative for this proposal? Or how attentive is this theology to the whole canon? After this, consider applying one principle from each of the other chapters. The key, again, is to start small and start somewhere. It would be exhausting to have to walk through *every* guiding principle in *every* chapter for *every* bit of theology one reads.

While all the principles are important, the hope is that over time applying these principles will become more and more intuitive as we become more skilled. There is no shortcut to developing skill. Skill requires practice, and practice in this case means reading lots and various types of theology. Practice also involves reading texts over and over again. At the very least, the seminal works in theology will require repeated interaction. Remember C. S. Lewis's description of the bad or "unliterary" reader: "The sure mark of an unliterary man is that he considers 'I've read it already' to be a conclusive argument against reading a work."[1] The literary person, by contrast, will read a text more than once to make sure he understands its many twists and turns.

Yet, alas, in the end we must make a judgment. I've heard it said that you should never critique someone until you are able to articulate their view as well as or better than they can.[2] While this sentiment is laudable and overlaps with the concerns of this book, applying it can also be quite crippling. It is doubtful that most readers—of theology or otherwise—will know another's argument better than that person does. And even in such cases, that type of knowledge takes time we often do not have. We must make a judgment *today*, even if it will likely be a *tentative* judgment. But that is okay. If we

---

1. C. S. Lewis, *Experiment in Criticism* (repr., Cambridge: Cambridge University Press, 2012), 2.
2. This sentiment is attributed to billionaire investor Charlie Munger.

remain open to correction, our convictions will not stifle our growth in knowledge. Allan Bloom has written that there are two kinds of openness: the openness of indifference and the openness that animates one's quest for knowledge and certitude. The first kind is unbounded, self-satisfied, and, ultimately, ambivalent to truth. "True openness," in contrast, "means closedness to all the charms that make us comfortable with the present."[3] This kind of openness lives in hope, the hope of gaining a deeper understanding of the truth than one has at present. In this light, we are free to make judgments, recognizing that they are provisional (i.e., they are true *as far as we know*). May this book serve as a catalyst for and a companion on your journey of love seeking critical understanding.

3. Allan Bloom, *The Closing of the American Mind*, Touchstone ed. (New York: Simon & Schuster, 1988), 41–42.

Index